Anonymous

Occasional Addresses

Anonymous

Occasional Addresses

ISBN/EAN: 9783743328310

Manufactured in Europe, USA, Canada, Australia, Japa

Cover: Foto ©ninafisch / pixelio.de

Manufactured and distributed by brebook publishing software (www.brebook.com)

Anonymous

Occasional Addresses

This is one of an edition of one hundred and eighty-five copies printed from type for the Dunlap Society in the month of December, 1890.

Theo. L. DeVinne & Co.

OCCASIONAL ADDRESSES

PUBLICATIONS OF THE DUNLAP SOCIETY

1886–1887.

I. THE CONTRAST. A comedy by Royall Tyler, with an introduction by Thomas J. McKee.

II. THE FATHER, OR AMERICAN SHANDYISM. A comedy by William Dunlap, with an introduction by Thomas J. McKee.

III. OPENING ADDRESSES. Edited by Laurence Hutton.

1888.

IV. ANDRÉ. A tragedy in five acts, by William Dunlap, with an introduction by Brander Matthews.

V. THOMAS ABTHORPE COOPER. A memoir of his professional life, by Joseph Norton Ireland.

VI. Biennial reports of the treasurer and secretary of the Dunlap Society.

1889.

VII. BRIEF CHRONICLES, by William Winter. Part I.
VIII. BRIEF CHRONICLES, by William Winter. Part II.
IX. CHARLOTTE CUSHMAN. A lecture by Lawrence Barrett, with an appendix containing a letter from Joseph N. Ireland.

1890.

X. BRIEF CHRONICLES, by William Winter. Part III.
XI. JOHN GILBERT. A sketch of his life, together with extracts from his letters and souvenirs of his career, by William Winter.
XII. OCCASIONAL ADDRESSES. Edited by Laurence Hutton and William Carey.

THE OLD ASTOR PLACE OPERA HOUSE
(DEMOLISHED 1890).

OCCASIONAL ADDRESSES

EDITED BY

LAURENCE HUTTON
AND
WILLIAM CAREY

NEW-YORK
THE DUNLAP SOCIETY
1890

918
H985
oc

Introduction.

THE present volume is a natural sequel to the collection of "Opening Addresses" published by The Dunlap Society in 1887. It is of necessity incomplete, the editors, out of the great mass of material at their command, having given preference to those Prologues, Epilogues, and other "Occasional Addresses" in verse with which the students of dramatic literature are least familiar. Many of the selections have appeared only in the periodical press, and a great number of them are published now for the first time.

The arrangement has been made chronological as far as is possible from the incomplete records that exist; and, as in the earlier volume, each address is prefaced by the names of its author and its speaker, together with the time and the place of its delivery.

The frontispiece is a reproduction, which is here published for the first time, of a drawing made by Mr. Roger Riordan for The Century Magazine. It shows *various views of the building on Astor Place, New York City, which was erected by subscription in 1847 and called the "Astor Place Opera House." Here it was that Macready appeared in 1848, and the street in front of this building, at the close of his performance, was the scene of the Macready Riot. In 1853 the building passed into the possession of the Mercantile Library Association. It was demolished in 1890.*

The editors wish to acknowledge their obligations to Mr. William Winter, Mr. George Parsons Lathrop, Mr. Brander Matthews, Mr. Henry Edwards, Mr. L. W. Kingman, Mr. Augustin Daly, Mr. Thomas Nelson Page, Mr. William L. Keese, Mr. William J. Henderson, Mr. J. M. Thompson, and Mr. George H. Jessop, for aid extended in the preparation of this volume.

LAURENCE HUTTON.
WILLIAM CAREY.

New-York, December, 1890.

Table of Contents.

		PAGE
1773. JOHN STREET THEATER, NEW-YORK	*Myles Cooper*	1
1778. BOW STREET THEATER, PORTSMOUTH, NEW HAMPSHIRE	*Jonathan M. Sewall*	4
1797. JOHN STREET THEATER, NEW-YORK	*Mr. Milne*	7
1823. THEATER, BOSTON	*Charles Sprague*	9
1823. PARK THEATER, NEW-YORK	*Joseph D. Fay*	17
1824. NEW AMERICAN THEATER, NEW ORLEANS	*Thomas Wells*	19
1825. NEW AMERICAN THEATER, NEW ORLEANS		22
1825. CHATHAM GARDEN THEATER, NEW-YORK	*Mrs. Entwistle*	24
1826. THEATER, HUNTSVILLE, ALABAMA		27
1829. NEW PARK THEATER, NEW-YORK	*Prosper M. Wetmore*	30
1829. NEW PARK THEATER, NEW-YORK	*James Lawson*	32
1830. NEW PARK THEATER, NEW-YORK	*Samuel Woodworth*	34
1830. NEW PARK THEATER, NEW-YORK		37
1831. CHATHAM THEATER, NEW-YORK	*Samuel Woodworth*	41

Table of Contents

		PAGE
1831. Park Theater, New-York	*Mr. Bailey*	44
1832. Theater, Cincinnati	*Caroline Lee Hentz*	46
1832. Park Theater, New-York	*Richard Penn Smith*	49
1833. Park Theater, New-York	*George P. Morris*	51
1833. Bowery Theater, New-York	*Samuel Woodworth*	54
1834. Histrionic Hall, Albany, New-York	*Charles Woodhouse*	57
1834. New Orleans	*George C. Chase*	59
1835. Park Theater, New-York	*George P. Morris*	61
1835. Theater, Albany, New-York	*Hugh Moore*	65
1837. New Theater, St. Louis, Mo.	*Edward Johnson*	67
1840. Amphitheater, Albany, New-York	*Alfred B. Street*	71
1851. Burton's Theater, New-York	*Henry Oake Pardey*	73
1852. Green Street Theater, Albany	*Julia de Marguerittes*	76
1855. Laura Keene's Varieties, New-York		77
1858. Academy of Music, Philadelphia	*Mr. Conrad*	79
1863. New Theater, Richmond, Va	*Henry Timrod*	82
1870. Fifth Avenue Theater, New-York	*William Winter*	87
1871. Wallack's Theater, New-York Fifth Avenue Theater, New-York Niblo's Theater, New-York Academy of Music, New-York	*George Vandenhoff*	91
1871. Opera House, Providence, R. I.	*C. C. Van Zandt*	94

Table of Contents.   xvii

			PAGE
1873.	New Park Theater, Brooklyn..................	William Winter.......	98
1873.	Fifth Avenue Theater, New-York..............	Oliver Wendell Holmes.	102
1874.	Booth's Theater, New-York....................	Richard Henry Stoddard	108
1875.	Fifth Avenue Theater, New-York..............	John Brougham........	112
1877.	Baldwin's Opera House, San Francisco, Cal...	George H. Jessop......	113
1878.	Grand Opera House, San Francisco, Cal......	Daniel O'Connell.....	118
1886.	Daly's Theater, New-York....Augustin Daly........		121
1886.	Star Theater, New-York.....George Parsons Lathrop.		124
1887.	Manchester, Mass ....T. W. Ball		126
1888.	Daly's Theater, New-York...Edgar Fawcett........		128
1888.	Manchester, Mass............T. W. Ball..........		132
1888.	The Players, New-York......Thomas W. Parsons..		134
1889.	Daly's Theater, New-York....William Winter......		136
1890.	Lyceum Theater, New London, Conn..............	George Parsons Lathrop.	137

3

Occasional Addresses

AN ADDRESS.

July 26, 1773.

Written by Reverend Doctor Myles Cooper for a benefit for the New-York Hospital. Spoken by Mr. Lewis Hallam at the John Street Theater, New-York.

WITH melting breast the wretch's pangs to feel,
His cares to soften, or his anguish heal;
Woe into peace by pity to beguile,
And make disease, and want, and sorrow smile;
Are deeds that nobly mark the generous mind
Which swells with liberal love to human kind,
And triumphs in each joy to others known
As blissful portions added to his own.
    Small though our powers, we pant with honest heart
In pity's cause to bear a humble part;
We gladly give *this night* to aid a plan
Whose object 's charity and good to man.
    Patrons of charity!   While time endures
Be every bliss of conscious virtue yours!
The hoary father, snatch'd from want and pain,
Oft to his consort and his youthful train

Shall praise the hand that rais'd his drooping head
When every hope, when every friend had fled,
That rais'd him, cold and naked, from the ground,
And pour'd the healing balsam in his wound;
With kindly art detain'd his parting breath,
And back repell'd the threat'ning dart of death.
The plaintive widow, shedding tears of joy,
As fondly watching o'er her darling boy,
Her anxious eyes, with keen discernment, trace
The dawn of health re'lumining his face,
Shall clasp him to her breast with raptures new,
And pour the prayer of gratitude for you.
In you, the long-lost characters shall blend,
Of guardian, brother, father, husband, friend!
And sure if bliss in mortal breast can shine,
That purest bliss, humanity! is thine.

   Let not mistaken avarice deplore
Each mite diminish'd from his useless store,—
But tell the wretch — that liberal acts bestow
Delights which hearts like his can never know.
Tell — for you feel — that generous love receives
A double portion of the joy it gives,
Beams o'er the soul a radiance pure and even,
And antedates on earth the bliss of Heaven.

   This night, to youth, our moral scene displays
How false, how fatal, are the wanton's ways;
Paints her alluring looks, fallacious wiles,
And the black ruin lurking in her smiles;—
Bids us the first approach of vice to shun,—
And claims a tear for innocence undone.

   While scenes like this employ our humble stage,
We fondly hope your favors to engage;

Occasional Addresses.

No ribald page shall here admittance claim,
Which decency or virtue brands with shame:
No artful hint that wounds the virgin's ear,
No thought that modesty would blush to hear.
We ask no patronage — disclaim applause —
But while we act and speak in virtue's cause.
This is our aim — and while we this pursue,
We ne'er can fail of patronage from you.

EPILOGUE TO CATO.

1778. *Written by Jonathan M. Sewall, for the Bow Street Theater, Portsmouth, N. H.*

YOU see mankind the same in ev'ry age;
   Heroic fortitude, tyrannic rage,
Boundless ambition, patriotic truth,
And hoary treason, and untainted youth,
Have deeply mark'd all periods, and all climes;
The noblest virtues, and the blackest crimes.
   Britannia's daring sins, and virtues both,
Perhaps once mark'd the Vandal and the Goth.
And what now gleams with dawning ray at home,
Once blaz'd in full-orb'd majesty at Rome.
   Did Cæsar, drunk with pow'r and madly brave,
Insatiate burn, his country to enslave?
Did he for this, lead forth a servile host,
And spill the choicest blood that Rome could boast?
Our British Cæsar too has done the same,
And damn'd this age to everlasting fame.
Columbia's crimson'd fields still smoke with gore!
Her bravest heroes cover all the shore!
The flow'r of Britain too in martial bloom,
In one sad year sent headlong to the tomb!
   Did Rome's brave senate nobly strive t' oppose
The mighty torrent of domestic foes?

And boldly arm the virtuous few, and dare
The desp'rate perils of unequal war?
   Our senate too, the same bold deed has done,
And for a Cato, arm'd a Washington!
A chief in all the ways of battle skill'd,
Great in the council, glorious in the field!
Thy scourge, O Britain! and Columbia's boast,
The dread, and admiration of each host!
Whose martial arm, and steady soul, alone
Have made thy legions quake, thy empire groan,
And thy proud monarch tremble on his throne.
What now thou art, oh! ever may'st thou be,
And death the lot of any chief but thee!
We've had one Decius too, and Howe can say
Health, pardon, peace, George sends America!
Yet brings destruction for the olive-wreath,
For health contagion, and for pardon death.
In brave Fayette young Juba lives again,
And many a Marcus bleeds on yonder plain.
Like Pompey, Warren fell in martial pride,
And great Montgomery like Scipio dy'd!
In Green the hero, patriot, sage we see,
And Lucius, Juba, Cato, shine in thee!
When Rome received her last decisive blow,
Hadst thou, immortal Gates, been Cæsar's foe,
All perfect *discipline* had check'd his sway,
And thy superior *conduct* won the day.
Freedom had triumph'd on Pharsalian ground,
Nor Saratoga's heights been more renown'd!
Long as heroic deeds the soul enflame,
Eternal praise bold Stark will ever claim,
Who led thy glorious way, and gave thee half thy fame.

See persevering A** proudly scale
Canadia's Alpine hills, a second Hannibal!
In Cæsar's days had such a daring mind
With Washington's serenity been join'd
The tyrant then had bled, great Cato liv'd,
And Rome in all her majesty surviv'd.
What praise, what gratitude, are due to thee,
Oh brave, experienc'd, all-accomplish'd Lee!
The sword, the pen, thou dost alternate wield,
Nor Julius' self to thee would blush to yield.
And while Sempronius' bellowings stun the ear,
I see the traitor C—— his thunders hear,
" But all was false, and hollow, tho' his tongue
Dropt manna," with the garb of reason hung.
Ere long the wily Syphax may advance,
And Afric faith be verify'd in France,
How long, deluded by that faithless pow'r,
Will ye dream on, nor seize the golden hour?
In vain do ye rely on foreign aid,
By her own arm and heav'n's Columbia must be freed.
 Rise then, my countrymen! for fight prepare,
Gird on your swords, and fearless rush to war!
For your griev'd country nobly dare to die,
And empty all your veins for *Liberty*.
No pent-up Utica contracts your pow'rs,
But the whole boundless continent is yours!

Occasional Addresses.

AN ADDRESS.

June, 1797.   *Written by Mr. Milne. Spoken by Mrs. Lewis Hallam at the John Street Theater, New-York.*

THESE flattering plaudits cannot fail to raise
　A *wish* to merit such transcendent praise;
It can but be a *wish*, for ah! — my heart
Knows *merit* could not claim a thousandth part:
But, like the lavish hand of Heaven, you
Give largely, e'en though nothing should be due.
O'ercome with joy, my anxious, throbbing heart,
Disdaining all the little tricks of art,
Conceals those feelings in a grateful breast
Which *may* be *felt*, but *cannot* be *express'd*.
Time has now swept ten rolling years away,
Since flattering plaudits graced my first essay,
Young, giddy, rash, ambitious, and untaught,
You still caress'd, excusing many a fault;
With friendly hand safe led me through the way
Where lurking error watches to betray:
And shall I such advantages forego
With my consent? I frankly answer, no:
I may, through inadvertency, have stray'd,
But who by folly *never* was betray'd?
If e'er my judgment played the foolish part,
I acted not in concert with my heart.

I boldly can defy the world to say
From my first entrée to the present day,
Whate'er my errors, numerous or few,
I never wanted gratitude to you.
On your indulgence still I 'll rest my cause;
Will you support me with your kind applause?
You verify the truth of Pope's fine line —
" To err is human; to forgive, divine."

AN ADDRESS.

1823. *Written by Mr. Charles Sprague, and read by Mr. Henry James Finn at an exhibition of a Pageant in Honor of Shakspeare at the Boston Theater.*

GOD of the glorious Lyre!
  Whose notes of old on lofty Pindus rang,
 While Jove's exulting choir
 Caught the glad echoes and responsive sang —
  Come! bless the service and the shrine
  We consecrate to thee and thine.

  Fierce from the frozen North,
  When havoc led his legions forth,
O'er Learning's sunny groves the dark destroyer spread;
  In dust the sacred statue slept,
  Fair Science round her altars wept,
   And Wisdom cowled his head.

  At length, Olympian Lord of morn,
  The raven veil of night was torn.
   When, through golden clouds descending,
   Thou didst hold thy radiant flight
    O'er nature's lovely pageant bending,
   Till Avon rolled, all sparkling, to thy sight!

There, on its bank, beneath the mulberry's shade,
Wrapp'd in young dreams, a wild-eyed minstrel
    strayed;
  Lighting there and lingering long,
  Thou didst teach the bard his song;
  Thy fingers strung his sleeping shell,
And round his brows a garland curled;
  On his lips thy spirit fell,
And bade him wake, and warm the world!

  Then Shakspeare rose!
  Across the trembling strings
  His daring hand he flings,
    And, lo! a new creation glows!
There, clustering round, submissive to his will,
Fate's vassal train his high commands fulfil.

  Madness, with his frightful scream;
    Vengeance, leaning on his lance;
  Avarice, with his blade and beam;
    Hatred, blasting with a glance;
Remorse, that weeps; and Rage, that roars,
And Jealousy, that dotes, but dooms and murders
    yet adores.

  Mirth, his face with sunbeams lit,
Waking laughter's merry swell,
  Arm in arm with fresh-eyed Wit,
That waves his tingling lash, while Folly shakes his
    bell.

    Despair, that haunts the gurgling stream,
    Kissed by the virgin moon's cold beam,
    Where some lost maid wild chaplets wreathes,
    And, swan-like, there her own dirge breathes,
Then, broken-hearted, sinks to rest,
Beneath the bubbling waves, that shroud her maniac breast.

    Young Love, with eye of tender gloom,
    Now drooping o'er the hallowed tomb,
    Where his plighted victims lie,
    Where they met, but met to die;
    And now, when crimson buds are sleeping,
    Through the dewy arbor creeping,
Where beauty's child, the frowning world forgot,
    To youth's devoted tale is listening,
    Rapture on her dark lash glistening,
While fairies leave their cowslip cells, and guard the happy spot.

    Thus rise the phantom throng,
    Obedient to their Master's song,
And lead in willing chain the wondering soul along,
For other worlds war's Great One sighed in vain —
O'er other worlds see Shakspeare rove and reign!
The rapt magician of his own wild lay,
Earth and her tribes his mystic wand obey,
Old ocean trembles, thunder cracks the skies,
Air teems with shapes, and tell-tale specters rise;
Night's paltering hags their fearful orgies keep,
And faithless guilt unseals the lip of sleep:

Time yields his trophies up, and death restores
The moldered victims of his voiceless shores.
The fireside legend, and the faded page,
The crime that cursed, the deed that blessed an age —
All, all, come forth — the good to charm and cheer,
To scourge bold Vice, and start the generous tear;
With pictured Folly, gazing fools to shame,
And guide young Glory's foot along the path of fame.
  Lo! hand in hand,
  Hell's juggling sisters stand,
 To greet their victims from the fight;—
  Grouped on the blasted heath,
  They tempt him to the work of death,
 Then melt in air, and mock his wondering sight.
  In midnight's hallowed hour,
  He seeks the fatal tower,
 Where the lone raven, perched on high,
  Pours to the sullen gale
  Her hoarse prophetic wail,
 And croaks the dreadful moment nigh.
 See, by the phantom dagger led,
Pale, guilty thing,
  Slowly he steals with silent tread,
And grasps his coward steel to smite his sleeping king.
  Hark! 't is the signal bell,
  Struck by that bold and unsexed one,
  Whose milk is gall, whose heart is stone,
  His ear hath caught the knell —
   'T is done! 't is done!
  Behold him from the chamber rushing,
  Where his dead monarch's blood is gushing,

Look where he trembling stands,
Sad gazing there;
Life's smoking crimson on his hands,
And in his felon heart the worm of wild despair.

Mark the sceptered traitor slumbering!
　There flit the slaves of conscience round,
With boding tongue foul murders numbering;
　Sleep's laden portals catch the sound;
In his dream of blood for mercy quaking,
At his own dull scream behold him waking!
Soon that dream to fate shall turn,
For him the living furies burn;
For him the vulture sits on yonder misty peak,
And chides the lagging night, and whets her hungry beak.
Hark! the trumpet's warning breath
Echoes round the vale of death.
Unhorsed, unhelmed, disdaining shield,
The panting tyrant scours the field;
　Vengeance! he meets thy dooming blade!
The scourge of earth, the scorn of Heaven,
He falls! unwept and unforgiven,
　And all his guilty glories fade.
Like a crushed reptile in the dust he lies,
And Hate's last lightning quivers from his eyes!
　Behold yon crownless king —
　　Yon white-locked, weeping sire —
　Where Heaven's unpillar'd chambers ring,
　　And burst their streams of flood and fire!

He gave them all — the daughters of his love —
That recreant pair! — they drive him forth to rove;
    In such a night of woe,
    The cubless regent of the wood
    Forgets to bathe her fangs in blood,
      And caverns with her foe;
      Yet one was ever kind —
      Why lingers she behind?
O, pity! — view him by her dead form kneeling,
Even in wild frenzy holy nature feeling.
    His aching eyeballs strain
    To see those curtained orbs unfold,
      That beauteous bosom heave again;
    But all is dark and cold;
    In agony the father shakes;
      Grief's choking note
      Swells in his throat,
    Each withered heartstring tugs and breaks!
Round her pale neck his dying arms he wreathes,
And on her marble lips his last, his death kiss breathes.
Down! trembling wing — shall insect weakness keep
The sun-defying eagle's sweep?
    A mortal strike celestial strings,
    And feebly echo what a seraph sings?
    Who now shall grace the glowing throne
    Where, all unrivaled, all alone,
Bold Shakspeare sat, and looked creation through,
The minstrel monarch of the worlds he drew?

That throne is cold — that lyre in death unstrung,
On whose proud note delighted Wonder hung.

Yet Old Oblivion, as in wrath he sweeps,
One spot shall spare, the grave where Shakspeare
 sleeps.
Rulers and ruled in common gloom may lie,
But Nature's laureate bards shall never die.
Art's chiseled boast, and Glory's trophied shore
Must live in numbers, or can live no more.
While sculptured Jove some nameless waste may claim,
Still rolls the Olympic car in Pindar's fame;
Troy's doubtful walls in ashes passed away,
Yet frown on Greece in Homer's deathless lay;
Rome, slowly sinking in her crumbling fanes,
Stands all immortal in her Maro's strains:
So, too, yon giant empress of the isles,
On whose broad sway the sun forever smiles,
To Time's unsparing rage one day must bend,
And all her triumphs in her Shakspeare end!

  O thou! to whose creative power
  We dedicate the festal hour,
While Grace and Goodness round the altar stand,
Learning's anointed train, and Beauty's rose-lipped
 band —
Realms yet unborn, in accents now unknown,
Thy song shall learn, and bless it for their own.
Deep in the West, as Independence roves,
His banners planting round the land he loves,
Where nature sleeps in Eden's infant grace,
In time's full hand shall spring a glorious race:
Thy name, thy verse, thy language shall they bear,
And deck for thee the vaulted temple there.

Our Roman-hearted father broke
Thy parent empire's galling yoke,
But thou, harmonious monarch of the mind,
Around their sons a gentler chain shall bind :
Still o'er our land shall Albion's scepter wave,
And what her mighty Lion lost her mightier Swan shall save.

EPILOGUE TO THE RENEGADE.

Sept. 26, 1823. *Written by Mr. Joseph D. Fay. Spoken by Miss Johnson, at the Park Theater, New-York.*

WEARY of plots and murders, bloody strife,
  Of war's hoarse din, and all the martial life,
The mimic mask laid by, I'm called to say
Something, by way of epilogue, to this new play.
And first, ye angel fair, whose brilliant eyes
Can knock our poet down, or bid him rise;
Fling out your smiles, his sinking hopes elate,
One smile from you may stamp his future fate.
And you, immortals, dwelling far above,
Who wield the thunder like immortal Jove,
Ring the long peal, in this our poet's cause,
And flash good-natured lightning for applause.
And you, oh critics! whose word, like doctor's pill,
Hath power to damn or save — to cure or kill;
Lo! our poor bard, on trembling footsteps borne,
Lest his first daring feat may meet your scorn,
Disordered, waits, with bosom sore afraid,
To die of doctors, or live by doctors' aid;
One smile from you were worth a world of wealth —
May I report him to the Board of Health
As safe and sound — his fears gone by forever,
And no more symptoms of the yellow fever?

Oh praise! how sweet thy sound to human ear—
We women *love* thee, and the *men* revere!
For thee, the statesman quits his tranquil life —
For thee, the hero seeks the battle's strife.
Toiling for thee, Columbus left his home,
Through unknown seas, in search of worlds to roam.
Homer and Shakspeare wrote alone for thee.
Oh! shed thy bounties on our bard, and me.
When first the eaglet, at his sire's behest,
On untried pinions, leaves his parent nest,
Fluttering, he flies; but soon the bird of Jove,
On wings of thunder, seeks the courts above.
Just so the bard, when first he dares to fling
His untried fingers on the sacred string;
He falters — stops — and anxious looks around,
To see if others like the virgin sound.
And should he hear the enlivening voice of praise,
He strikes the harp to more majestic lays.
With bolder hand he sweeps the living lyre,
While thronging thousands listen and admire.

AN ADDRESS.

Jan. 1, 1824.
Written by Mr. Thomas Wells. Spoken by Mr. James H. Caldwell, at the opening of the New American Theater, New Orleans.

WHEN first, o'er Learning, Persecution trod,
And fettered Letters felt his iron rod,
Long, long in darkness bound, the Muses slept,
Each haunt left bardless, and each harp unswept;
'Till, bursting through the gloom, dramatic fire
Apollo darted o'er each slumbering lyre;
Through clouds of dullness shot his attic light,
And chased the shades of superstitious night;
Loud pæans then broke forth from every tongue,—
The Temples echoed, and the Chorus rung—
Warm with new soul, young Music smote the strings,
To Song gave life — to Inspiration wings!
Genius, by Freedom roused, shook off his yoke,
And from his deep, oblivious dream awoke!
Awoke, and saw the *Drama's* towering dome
Swell its asylum arch, and call him *home;*
Allured to *higher worlds*, he took his flight,
And rose to realms of *empyrean* height,
Explored the winding paths of Fiction's bowers,
And gathered for the *Stage* his *deathless* flowers.
Her ample page redeeming Learning spread,
And o'er the night of Mind her radiance shed,

Taste polished life — the arts refined the age —
And Virtue triumphed as she reared the Stage.
Patrons! this night our cause to you we trust,
As Guardians of the Drama's rights — be just;
Support from you the child of Thespis draws,
Warms in your sun, and thrives on your applause;
At your tribunal he expecting stands,
And craves indulgent judgment at your hands;
Your willing smiles then let his efforts share,
And, to your shelter take the buskin's heir!
O, let your *presence*, let your plaudits cheer
Our Protean toil, and give us welcome here!
And yet, no purchased favor we would ask;
Unbiased and unbought fulfil your task.
Before your critic-bench we humbly bend,
And to your righteous voice ourselves commend;
No servile suppliants to your court, we sue,
But praise and censure claim alike, from you;
Assembled here, to *your* decree submit,
And hail in you the arbiters of wit.
And, now, in scenic beauty drest, thou Dome —
The shield of Morals, and of Song the home —
The nurse of Eloquence — the school of Taste,
Hence be thy altars by the Muses graced.
Within thy walls, perhaps, by Genius led
Shall future Shakspeares sing, or Garricks tread;
In Roman grace, and majesty of mien,
Some Kemble reign, the monarch of the scene;
Her fire of soul some Siddons here impart,
Shoot through each quivering nerve, and storm the heart;

Occasional Addresses.

On rapid wing still speeds the auspicious time,
When bards our own the Olympic mount shall climb;
When round their consecrated shrines shall throng
Our buskined heroes, and *our* sons of *Song;*
In attic pride *our* Drama then shall rise,
And nobly daring, claim the Thespian prize:
To classic height exalt the rising age,
And give, to peerless, lasting fame, the Stage.

A PRIZE POEM.

Jan. 8, 1825. *Spoken by Mr. James H. Caldwell, at the New American Theater, New Orleans.*

CHILL was the breeze, nor yet the herald light
   Had chased the lingering shadows of the night;
O'er still expanse of lake, and marshy bed,
Gloomy and dense the mantling vapors spread:
But soon the battle-flash that darkness broke,
And soon, that dread repose, the peal awoke
Of loud artillery, and the dire alarms
Of mingling conflict, and the clash of arms.

  Fate gave the word! and now, by veterans led,
In pride of chivalry, to conquest bred,
The foe advanced — entrenched, the champion band
Of freemen stood, the bulwark of the land;
Fearless their stars unfurled, and, as the rock,
Storm-proof, they stood, impervious to the shock:
Their patriot *Chief* — with patriot ardor fired —
Nerved every hand, and every heart inspired;
Himself, in peril's trying hour, a host:
A nation's rescue, and a nation's boast.

As near the bastion'd wall the invader drew,
A storm of iron hail to greet him flew;
On Havoc's wing the mission'd vengeance rode,
And whole platoons the scythe of Ruin mowed;
Through paths of blood, o'er undistinguished slain,
Unyoked, the hungry war-dogs scoured the plain:
Borne on the blast, the scattering besom kept
Its course, and ranks on ranks promiscuous swept.
The trophied *Lion* fell — while o'er his foes
Unscathed, in arms supreme, the towering *Eagle* rose.

Sublime in majesty — matchless in might —
Columbia stood, unshaken in the fight;
From lips of adamant, 'midst volumed smoke
And cataracts of fire, her thunders spoke
In triumph to the skies; from shore to shore
Old Mississippi shook, and echoed to the roar.

High on his sceptered perch, our mountain bird
Amidst the din the shout of Victory heard,
Exulting heard, and from his aery came
Through clouds of rolling dun, and sheets of flame;
Renown's immortal meed he bore, and spread
His ample pinions o'er the conqueror's head —
THE HERO OF THE WEST — to him assigned
The glorious palm, and round his brows the guerdon twined.

A RIFLEMAN'S ADDRESS.

July 23, 1825.   *Written by "George." Spoken by Mrs. Entwistle, at the Chatham Garden Theater, New-York.*

WHERE sinks the sun in majesty to rest,
    Within the bosom of the bonny West;
Where roves the hunter, where the forest blooms,
And where the rose the ambient air perfumes;
Where lakes and hills diversify the earth,
With patriot kinsmen I received my birth.
In sex a woman — yet a man in nerve —
In wish a warrior, this proud land to serve;
My greatest boast is in my rifle's aim,
In God, my honor, and my country's fame.
For her I deal my tomahawk's dread blow,
To send destruction on her ruthless foe;
For her the knife and polished sword I draw,
To shield her rights and vindicate her law.
The ardent flame which in this bosom glows,
In former days with Washington arose:
Oh, who can dwell upon that hallowed name,
Inscribed by glory on the roll of fame;
Nor feel his heart with adoration beat
For him who braved the fiercest battle's heat?

'Mid war, and danger, and the worst of griefs,
He stood the bravest and the best of chiefs.
Then strive each patriot — father, brother, son —
To imitate the peerless Washington.
But while we ponder on the time that's fled,
"The army's idol, and the council's head,"
Oh, can we then, my countrymen, forget
The brave, the honored, noble Lafayette?
No, by the stream that circles in your veins,
While freedom's spark within this clime remains,
His name shall vibrate to the distant poles,
Long as a billow of the ocean rolls.
This is the language of the West — 't is mine —
And oh, my country, it was ever thine.
If War's hoarse throat should summon us again,
To drive the foeman from our native plain;
Led on by Jackson, will our hardy band,
Like heroes struggle for their native land;
And while his presence animates the field,
The eagle to the kite shall never yield.
Enough of war! that gentle, blue-eyed maid,
Celestial Peace — in spotless garb arrayed —
Her choicest blessings o'er our soil she flings,
And sheds pure crystal from her downy wings:
She drives her chariot over hill and plain,
With Wealth and Commerce in her happy train;
Brown Agriculture and the Arts convene,
To pause and ponder on the grateful scene;
While Science moves with stately steps along,
With blushing Genius and the Child of Song.

Oh happy country! on this hallowed day,
Ere half a century moved its course away,
Thy sons the banner of our land unfurled,
And published freedom to a startled world;
The crown, the scepter, and the tyrant's yoke,
With manly strength the mighty warriors broke,
And taught the rulers of the land and sea
Columbia would — Columbia must be free!

AN ADDRESS.

July 24, 1826. *Spoken by Mr. James H. Caldwell, at the opening of the Theater, Huntsville, Alabama.*

IN climes of the East, when dark Tyranny's form
Rode in triumph aloft, on proud Victory's storm,
The genius of Freedom in agony wept
O'er the tomb where the martyr of liberty slept.
Their relics in silent devotion she blest,
Then sought an asylum in climes of the West;
On the plains of Columbia her stripes were unfurl'd,
And here she spoke thunders to tyranny's world!
The conflict o'er, the warring discords hush'd,
The tyrant fall'n, and his minions crush'd,
Oppression's requiem o'er his tomb is hung,
And Freedom's triumph in hosannas sung!
When the dread trumpet of the battle closed,
And fair Columbia safe in peace reposed;
The gleam of science in effulgence glowed
On the wild land of Liberty's abode.
'T was here that once the wandering Indian stray'd
Or slothful slumbered in the sylvan shade;
Quafied the clear streamlet as it pour'd along,
Or sung the burden of his heathen song;
His home — the valley — or the mountain cave,
The dreary forest — or the restless wave.

To bask unthoughtful in the morning's beam,
Or trace the windings of the rolling stream,
Or vie in swiftness with the fleetest hind,
Was the rich glory of the savage mind.

But see how changed the Alabama's plain,
And how transformed are all its roving train;
See Learning rising from the sage's dome,
And beams in brightness o'er the heathen's home;
See Mind emerging from its moral night,
And claim its lineage from the " throne of light."
And here, behold! the Drama's temple rise
In the bright beauty of its varied dyes;
May circling halos round its summit gleam,
And bursting visions round its altars stream;
May Fancy *here*, on waving pinions fly,
And pour her light from every star on high.
Oh! fostering genius of the rising stage
Display the treasures of thy classic page,
And here, oh! let the infant drama claim
Thy glow celestial, and thy radiant flame;
Here let the tragic and the comic muse,
Mingle their crimson and their airy hues;
Disclose their horrors, or the hero's doom,
And weep in sorrow o'er the bloody tomb.
Here let young passion at thy altar stand;
But own the presence of stern reason's hand;
Improve his feelings, purify their flow,
Curb his loose fires, but let his ardor glow.
And here let knowledge, dignified and chaste,
And truth and virtue, elegance and taste,

Exclusive wit, amusive and refin'd,
Unfold their splendor to the youthful mind.
Let mingling beauties round this circle move,
Like a bright vision in the dream of love,
And youth and wisdom, innocence and age,
Feast on the pleasures of the polished stage.

PROLOGUE TO METAMORA.

Dec. 15, 1829. *Written by Mr. Prosper M. Wetmore. Spoken by Mr. Barrett, New Park Theater, New-York.*

NOT from the records of Imperial Rome,
  Or classic Greece — the muses' chosen home —
From no rich legends of the olden day
Our bard hath drawn the story of his play;
Led by the guiding hand of genius on,
He here hath painted Nature on her throne;
His eye hath pierced the forest's shadowy gloom,
And read strange lessons from a nation's tomb:
Brief are the annals of that blighted race —
These halls usurp a monarch's resting-place —
Tradition's mist-enshrouded page alone
Tells that an empire was — we know 't is gone!
  From foreign climes full oft the muse hath brought
Her glorious treasures of gigantic thought;
And here, beneath the witchery of her power,
The eye hath poured its tributary shower:
When modern pens have sought th' historic page,
To picture forth the deeds of former age —
O'er soft Virginia's sorrows ye have sighed,
And dropt a tear when spotless beauty died;
When Brutus " cast his cloud aside "; to stand
The guardian of the tyrant-trampled land —

When patriot Tell his clime from thraldom freed,
And bade th' avenging arrow do its deed,
Your bosoms answered with responsive swell,
For freedom triumphed when th' oppressors fell!
   These were the melodies of humbler lyres,
The lights of Genius, yet without his fires;
But when the master-spirit struck the chords,
And inspiration breathed her burning words —
When passion's self stalked living o'er the stage,
To plead with love, or rouse the soul to rage —
When Shakspeare led his bright creations forth,
And conjured up the mighty dead from earth —
Breathless — entranced — ye 've listened to the line,
And felt the minstrel's power, all but divine!
   While thus your plaudits cheer the stranger lay,
Shall native pens in vain the field essay?
To-night we test the strength of native powers,
Subject, and bard, and actor, all are ours —
'T is yours to judge, if worthy of a name,
And bid them live within the halls of fame!

EPILOGUE TO METAMORA.

Dec. 15, 1829. *Written by Mr. James Lawson. Spoken by Mrs. Hilson, New Park Theater, New-York.*

BEFORE this bar of beauty, taste, and wit,
This host of critics, too, who throng the pit,
A trembling bard has been this night arraigned;
And I am counsel in the cause retained.
Here come I, then, to plead with nature's art,
And speak, less to the law, than to the heart.
   A native bard — a native actor too,
Have drawn a native picture to your view;
In fancy, this bade Indian wrongs arise,
While that embodied all before your eyes;
Inspired by genius, and by judgment led,
Again the Wampanoag fought and bled;
Rich plants are both of our own fruitful land,
Your smiles the sun that made their leaves expand;
Yet, not that they are native do I plead,
'T is for their worth alone I ask your meed.
How shall I ask ye? Singly? Then I will —
But should I fail? Fail! I must try my skill.
   Sir, I know you — I 've often seen your face,
And always seated in that selfsame place;
Now, in my ear — what think you of our play?
That it has merit truly, he did say;

And that the hero, prop'd on genius' wing,
The Indian forest scoured, like Indian king!
  See that fair maid, the tear still in her eye,
And hark! hear not you now that gentle sigh?
Ah! these speak more than language could relate,
The woe-fraught heart o'er Nahmeokee's fate;
She scans us not by rigid rules of art,
Her test is feeling, and her judge the heart.
  What dost thou say, thou bushy-whiskered beau?
He nods approval — whiskers are the go.
  Who is he sits the fourth bench from the stage?
There; in the pit! — why he looks wond'rous sage!
He seems displeased, his lip denotes a sneer —
O! he 's a critic that looks so severe!
Why, in his face I see the attic salt —
A critic's merit is to find a fault.
What fault find you, sir? eh! or you, sir? None!
Then, if the critic 's mute, my cause is won.
Yea, by that burst of loud heartfelt applause,
I feel that I have gained my client's cause.
Thanks, that our strong demerits you forgive,
And bid our bard and Metamora live.

EPILOGUE TO NARRAH MATTAH.

Jan. 15, 1830.   *Written by Mr. Samuel Woodworth. Delivered by Mrs. Sharp at New Park Theater, New-York.*

THE curtain 's down; and, while they 're all behind
  Doffing their pilgrim dresses, I 've a mind
At the gay modern world to have one peep,
And just say, " How d' ye do ? " before I sleep.
But how is this ? Am I to understand
That these are the descendants of that band
Of pious plain-clad pilgrims, who came o'er
To seek for freedom on this Western shore ?
Why—where 's the plain mob cap ? the russet gown ?
The puritanic coat ? the close-cropt crown ?
Where 's all that neat simplicity of dress
Which marked the Puritans ? Egad ! I guess
I wa' n't alone—more of them must have wed
With native chiefs, and mingled white and red ;
Else why this taste for feathers, beads, and shells,
In their descendants ? Why do modern belles
Paint their sweet faces, and from either ear
Suspend those sparkling trinkets ? And then here
So modestly to bury half their charms
In those huge silken bags that hide their arms ?

O there 's red blood in some of your blue veins,
And so there is in yours, ye dapper swains,
Or what 's the meaning of those dandy chains
Extending from your bosoms to your pockets?
I wonder if you modern beaux wear lockets!
Nay, hope not to escape me — you will fail,
Those treacherous square-toes, I shall know your trail
I see you there, but I won't tell your name,
He with the whiskers — yes — that 's him — the same
A mighty chief of some great tribe, no doubt,
You need not tell me — I shall make it out:
Yes, yes — I see — it plainly now appears,
Those artificial whiskers hide long ears!
But he with that blue blanket on one shoulder,
And feathered lip, must be a chief still bolder;
Perhaps a sachem, sagamore, or scribe,
O I perceive, he 's of the cockney tribe.

    But what is that thing? — yonder — up above?
He with the eye-glass? There! he 's dropt his glove;
What tribe claims him — or it — that taper shape?
I 've strong suspicions it must be the ape!

    You need n't smile, here, in the pit, below,
For I 've a word with you before I go.
Yes, do smile! In mercy don't look grave,
For 't is your tribe must either damn or save
The little bantling just gone off the stage.
Forget its faults, but not its tender age.
What if it be a little rude and wild,
Remember that a parent loves his child;
And I 'll be sworn he 's somewhere here to-night,
With feelings none can know but they who write.

So be good-natured, now, ye critic tribe;
Nay, do not frown — can I not name some bribe?
Yes, here it goes — don't let the new play fall,
And Narrah Mattah vows to kiss you all.

'T is safe! 't is safe! your generous hands decide it;
There, take a kiss among you, and divide it.

EPILOGUE TO ROKEBY.

May, 1830.   *Spoken by Barnes, Placide, and Hilson. Delivered at the New Park Theater, New-York.*

BARNES.— O, spare your hands — 't is useless all this blarney;
The play can't live, without a word from Barney;
'T is like a patient — quacks to death may steam him,
And he is damned, if science don't redeem him.
Grappling with fate 't is I alone can part 'em,
Barney will save the piece, *secundem artem*.

   Go on, that 's right, your smiles are what I 'm after,
The best prescription is a roar of laughter;
One hearty laugh, no matter how excited,
May save a life when every hope is blighted.

   'T is true, Placide has got an epilogue,
But 't ain't the thing — it don't " go the whole hog ";
So, while he 's back there, spelling out each line,
I 'll give you an *extrumpery* of mine;
Original throughout — no one has read it —
So, if you have a tear, " prepare to shed it ":

   A certain fair one — once, in days of yore,
Caught a bad quinsey, and her throat was sore;
She could not speak, nor swallow, chew, nor sup,
She scarcely breathed — the doctors gave her up.

Her weeping friends, in silence, breathed their sighs,
And stood prepared to close her fading eyes!
'T was at this awful crisis, 'mid the gloom,
Her favorite monkey stole into the room;
With doctor's formal air approached the bed,
Seized hold her wrist, then gravely shook his head.
The droll manœuver called a smile from death,
And one convulsive laugh restored her breath,
Broke her disorder, let the fair escape,
Who owed her cure alone to Dr. Ape:

D' ye take? or must I give your wits a jog?
Stay — here comes Harry with his epilogue.

PLACIDE.— "In ancient times, when plighted vows were broken —"
BARNES.— You 're too late, Hal, the epilogue is spoken.
PLACIDE.— Spoken! By whom?
BARNES.— By me.
PLACIDE.— By you?
BARNES.— 'T is certain.
PLACIDE.— Why, 't is n't a minute since they dropt the curtain,
And my address a good half hour employs.
BARNES.— " I 've done the deed — didst thou not hear a noise?"
If you attempt, you 'll find yourself mistaken;
I made them laugh — that saved the author's bacon.
PLACIDE.— And who, pray, bade you show your monkey capers?
The sun requires no aid from farthing tapers —
I saved the piece, sir.

BARNES.— You?
PLACIDE.— My humble talents
  Secured the thing's success and turned the balance,
  Or, as Prince Rupert says — "Alone I did it!"
  It 's true, I pledge my honor!
HILSON.— Heaven forbid it!
  To put so mean a trifle " up the spout "!
PLACIDE.— Hilson, be quiet! I know what I 'm
  about.
HILSON.— That tone, my boy, smacks sharply of the
  acid.
BARNES.— Placide, by name, but not exactly placid.
  You 're somewhat wroth.
PLACIDE.— I am, and shall be wrother.
  I 'll speak my speech!
HILSON.— Not if you love the author.
  Since I have saved his opera, 't were wrong
  To jeopardize it with a speech so long.
PLACIDE.— You saved the opera!
BARNES.— You saved it!
BOTH.— You!
HILSON.— Yes, I myself alone — you know it 's
  true;
  I hit it on the head — but lest it fail,
  Here 's a short epilogue to clench the nail;
    " When erst the Muses on Parnassus' top,
  In mazy dances —"
BARNES.— Prithee, Tommy, stop;
  Throw poetry and physic to the dogs,
  Nor bore our friends, here, with dull epilogues.
HILSON.— Agreed, old Barney! and to end disputes,
  The readiest way to harmonize our flutes,

Is to admit — so be it understood,
To please our friends we 've all done what we could.
If we have failed —
PLACIDE.— Why then —
BARNES.— What then, Placide?
PLACIDE.— They 'll take "a good intention for the deed."
HILSON.— I 'll answer for 't — I know these generous folks,
They 're always laughing at us, or our jokes;
But what of our young author? Jests nor wit
Won't add a penny to his benefit.
PLACIDE.— His benefit is safe.
BARNES.— What then of Rokeby?
HILSON.— Should that be damn'd, it would a serious joke be.
But see! there 's mercy in each judge's eye —
The bard 's acquitted! — Rokeby shall not die!
PLACIDE.— Egad, their plaudits make old Drury shake.
HILSON.— It 's just the thing!
BARNES.— I say — " there 's no mistake!"

EPILOGUE TO OSWALI.

June 6, 1831. *Written by Mr. Samuel Woodworth. Spoken by Mrs. Hughes at the Chatham Theater, New-York.*

DON'T be alarm'd because you saw me slain,
And now behold me on the stage again;
For you must know, we murder here "*in jest*";
But had it been in *earnest*, could I rest
In quiet, think ye, even in the grave,
When my appearance Oswali might save?
You know how cleverly I rush'd between
The youth and fate — there, in my dying scene;
And if I fell a martyr for him there,
In the same cause I 've yet some breath to spare.

My turban'd Turkish tyrant lover said,
That I, among the dying and the dead,
When Moslem wrath its bolts of vengeance hurl'd,
"*Hung like an angel o'er a blazing world.*"
'T was most gallantly spoken for a Turk,
The ruthless author of that bloody work;
What then, ye free-born Christians, ought to be
Your exclamation — when you witness me
Rise from the bier to intercede for one,
Whom you are proud to call "Columbia's son";
For, though no stoics, you will not disdain
To own the pleasure you 've derived from *Payne*.

'T is not in ghostly costume I appear —
No bullet wound — no crimson stain is here,.
I 'm not a *shade*, or *specter*, good or evil —
Nor am I quite an *angel*, or a *devil;*
No spirit of the air — or fire — or flood —
But true substantial *female* flesh and blood;
Disclaiming powers and titles superhuman,
Though a true *patriot*, I am still a *woman;*
As such, I love the youth who freely fights
For country — freedom — and for female rights;
As such, I come to plead our poet's cause,
And ask a verdict in your kind applause.

Why do *you* smile, there — Mr. Zoilus — say —
I know you well — *you* once produced a play,
And said we *actors* damn'd it! — let that pass —
Bards *must* be civil when their house is glass.

And *you*, Sir Critic — who one night — don't start —
Assum'd the buskin — and — *forgot your part!*
You 'll be indulgent, won't you? nay, for shame!
Don't look so frighten'd — I 'll not tell your name.

Ay, there is sunshine in this sparkling crescent;
Those smiling faces promise something pleasant.
Were Payne but here, how he would idolize
This starry galaxy of laughing eyes!
Who 's he that sits behind yon lady? — Pshaw!
That mammoth hat! — what *do* you wear it for?
Why not confine your ringlets, puffs and curls
In a neat turban, like our Grecian girls?

There are some eyes behind that monstrous screen
That might smile kindly — could they but be seen.
Egad! — I 've caught one! — thank you — that's enough —
You 're on the *free-list*, sir, and we expect a *puff*.

To you who choose a more exalted station,
We look with confidence for approbation;
For *elevated* souls, in every age,
Have been the friends of genius and the stage;
And never be it said, that our own Payne
Pleaded for mercy to the *gods* in vain.

EPILOGUE TO WALDEMAR.

NOV. 1, 1831.   *Written by Mr. Bailey. Spoken by Mrs. Sharpe at the Park Theater, New-York.*

IT *must* be done. The man's heart will be broken
Unless some sort of epilogue be spoken;
Besides, the house expects it — always — don't you?
I'm sure you'll let me try one for him — won't you?
Only a word — to help along the play?
The author's almost scared to death, they say.
To leave him thus would be, indeed, a sin —
Come, " down in front," " hats off," and I'll begin.

When the young rose first opens in the vale,
Its bud, uncurling, scarcely scents the gale.
Should chilling winds and angry storms arise,
It droops its leaves, and prematurely dies.
But, let the sun inspire each tender charm,
Cheer it with smiles, with melting kisses warm,
Grateful it blooms — preserved from early death,
And thanks the heavens with its ambrosial breath.
And so, the author, trembling, first appears,
Nurses one hope amid a thousand fears;
Starts lest he mark some awful symptom lower,
(A sensitive plant — your literary flower).

This is *his* sky — and mine the task to find —
Must he be withered with the wintry wind?
Will he meet stormy weather here, I wonder?
Did n't you think you heard a clap of thunder?

You wicked critics — ranged around, that sit,
With your stop-watches, yonder, in the pit;
Whose dreams are haunted, for your faces show it,
With the dim ghosts of many a murdered poet,
Shall I our author's thronging doubts allay?
May I inform him that you like his play?
Will ye be civil?   Will ye take his hand,
And cheer his way o'er fancy's fairy-land?
Will you hie home, and, by your midnight tapers,
Do "the genteel thing" for him in the papers?
Or strive, like Shylock, though in style politer,
To "cut the forfeit" from a bankrupt writer?

To you I turn, th' Apollos and the Graces,
And read indulgence in your smiling faces.
None here the generous tribute will refuse,
Wooed by a native author's early muse.
Anxious he waits, as one who from a steep
Watches his vessel launched upon the deep.
With you it rests th' adventurous bark to save;
Let not his hard-earned treasures feed the wave.
O'er the blue sea a summer's calmness throw,
Bid prosperous breezes swell the sails of snow.
Let him but once your generous favor share,
And then, ye critics, touch him if ye dare.

AN ADDRESS.

July 4, 1832. *Written by Mrs. Caroline Lee Hentz. Spoken by Mr. James H. Caldwell at the opening of the New Theater at Cincinnati.*

WHAT Grecian dome o'ertopp'd its gates of pride
  In more auspicious hour? The eventide
Of freedom's most august and glorious day
Pours on these classic walls its hallowed ray,
And the rich gale, that now floats wearied by,
Has borne a nation's gratitude on high.
While from the fountain of each patriot heart
Gushes of high, heroic feeling start,
The children of the free, we gather here,
Anthems of glory lingering in our ear,
To dedicate this yet unsullied shrine,
By rites the bards of old believed divine.
When first the strain that still from clime to clime
Rolls its deep echoes down the flood of time
Swell'd o'er our ancient hills, gray rocks, and green-
    wood bowers
Show'd *this* fair city, *then*, its stately towers?
No! Nature here in druid grandeur dwelt,
Before her throne the forest monarch knelt,

Faith's only altar, earth's vine-shadowed foam,
And God's sole temple yon unchiseled dome.
But Freedom traveling in its strength unfurl'd
Erewhile its banner o'er this western world —
Religion, science, genius, wealth, and taste,
Followed with gliding steps the path she trac'd,
Scatter'd the stars amid the forest gloom,
And gave to man the wild's uncultur'd bloom.
Here, too, the Muses, seraph pilgrims, came,
Heralds and guardians of the drama's fame —
Whose lyre, from land to land, from age to age,
Has wak'd its noblest descant for the stage.
Hail to this shrine! Oh! never may the flame
Enkindled here be dimmed by clouds of shame —
May sorrow gather here, a thornless flower,
Whose bloom shall sweeten life's autumnal hour;
Virtue, oppressed by passion's lawless rage,
Find an avenging champion in the stage,
And conscience, writhing in conviction's grasp,
Pierc'd by remorse, with pangs, convulsive gasp.
Patrons of genius! be it yours to guard
This virgin temple, spotless and unmarr'd,
High o'er its gates inscribe this ban to sin,
Let not pollution dare to enter in.
Then even prayer in holy brow may bend,
And bless the drama, as religion's friend.
May native genius, sunning in the ray
Your smiles reflect, exalt its boldest lay,
And reaching here ambition's loftiest goal,
On glory's page your fathers' deeds enroll.

The bard, in vision, sees with prophet glance
The glimmering shades of other years advance,
Where fair Ohio's waves embalmed in song,
A second Avon flows in pride along,
And every regal mountain of the West
Lifts, with Olympian fame, its rainbow'd crest.
As erst the pilgrim to the hills of Rome,
To this proud dome unnumber'd votaries come;
And lingering o'er the annals of this day,
Dear to our country's pride, exulting say:
" Ye walls — corruption never has profan'd,
Long may ye stand unmoldering as unstain'd."

PROLOGUE TO ORALLOOSA.

Dec. 7, 1832. *Written by Mr. Richard Penn Smith. Spoken by Mr. Duffy, at the Park Theater, New-York.*

TO wake the mold'ring ashes of the dead,
And o'er forgotten ages light to shed,
Until the picture in such color glows
That truth approaches,— time his power foregoes;
T' anatomize the pulses of the soul,
From gentlest throb to throes beyond control;
The varied passion from their germ to trace,
Till reason totters from her judgment place;
To call the latent seeds of virtue forth,
And urge the mind to deeds of lasting worth.
For this the Stage in ancient days arose;
In teaching this she triumphed o'er her foes,
And soon became, in spite of bigot rule,
A nation's glory, and a nation's school.
Too long we 've been accustomed to regard
Alone the dogmas of some foreign bard.
Too long imagined, 'neath our shifting skies,
" That fancy sickens, and that genius dies."
Dreaming, when Freedom left old Europe's shore,
Spread the strong wing new regions to explore,
Her altar in the wilderness to raise
Where all might bend, and safely chaunt her praise,

Occasional Addresses.

The gifted nine refused to join her train,
And still amidst their ruined haunts remain.
Banish the thought; extend the fostering hand,
And wild-eye'd Genius soars at your command;
With " native wood-notes wild " our hills shall swell,
Till all confess the Muses with us dwell.
Our bard, to-night, a bold adventurer grown,
A flight has taken to the torrid zone:
Calls from the grave the ruthless Spaniard's dust,
To meet the judgment of the free and just,
Shows, in the progress of his mournful song,
The Indian's vengeance, and the Indian's wrong;
How bigots, with the cross and sword in hand,
Unpeopled and laid waste the peaceful land,
Then scourged the conquered with an iron rod,
And stabb'd for gold the seeming zeal for God!
Critics! a word! — we pray, be not too hard
On native actor or on native bard,
A second time th' offenders stand before you,
Therefore for mercy humbly we implore you,
When last arraigned the cause was ably tried,
For *Gladiators* battled on their side:
Took you by storm: ere you knew what to say
The valiant rogues had fairly won the day.
Should *Oralloosa* prove a victor too,
His triumph here repays for lost Peru.

AN ADDRESS.

February, 1833.
Written by Mr. George P. Morris. Spoken by Mrs. Sharpe, on the evening of the festival in honor of Mr. Dunlap, at the Park Theater, New-York.

WHAT gay assemblage greets my wondering sight?
    What scene of splendor — conjured here to-night?
What voices murmur, and what glances gleam?
Sure 't is some flattering, unsubstantial dream.
The house is crowded — everybody 's here
For beauty famous, or to science dear;
Doctors and lawyers, judges, belles and beaux,
Poets and painters — and heaven only knows
Whom else beside — and, see, gay ladies sit,
Lighting with smiles that fearful place, the pit
(A fairy change — ah, pray continue it).
Gray heads are here too, listening to my rhymes,
Full of the spirit of departed times;
Grave men and studious, strangers to my sight,
All gather round me on this brilliant night.
And welcome are ye all. Not now ye come
To speak some trembling poet's awful doom;
With frowning eyes a " want of mind " to trace
In some new actor's inexperienced face
Or e'en us old ones (oh, for shame!) to rate
" With study, good — in time — but — never great ";

Not like yon travel'd *native*, just to say
" Folks in this country cannot act a play,
They can't, 'pon honor!" How the creature starts!
His wit and *whiskers* came from foreign parts!
Nay, madam, spare your blushes — you I mean —
There — close beside him — oh, you 're full sixteen —
You need not shake your flowing locks at me —
The man, your sweetheart — then I 'm dumb, you see;
I 'll let him off — you 'll punish him in time,
Or I 've no skill in prophecy or rhyme;
Nor like that knot of surly critics yonder,
Who wield the press, that modern bolt of thunder,
To " cut us up," when from this house they lollop,
With no more mercy than fair *Mrs. Trollope!*
A nobler motive fills your bosoms now,
To wreath the laurel round the silver'd brow
Of one who merits it — if any can,
The artist, author, and the honest man.
With equal charms his pen and pencil drew
Rich scenes, to nature and to virtue true.
Full oft upon these boards hath youth appear'd,
And oft your smiles his faltering footsteps cheer'd;
But not alone on budding genius smile,
Leaving the ripen'd sheaf unown'd the while;
To boyish hope not every bounty give,
And only youth and beauty bid to live.
Will you forget the services long past,
Turn the old war-horse out to die at last?
When, his proud strength and noble fleetness o'er,
His faithful bosom dares the charge no more?

Ah, no — the sun that loves his beams to shed
Round every opening flowret's tender head,
With smiles as kind his genial radiance throws
To cheer the sadness of the fading rose.
Thus he, whose merit claims this dazzling crowd,
Points to the past, and has his claims allowed;
Looks brightly forth, his faithful journey done,
And rests in triumph — like the setting sun.

AN ADDRESS.

Nov. 7, 1833.
Written by Mr. Samuel Woodworth on the benefit of Mr. Thomas A. Cooper. Spoken by Mr. Thomas Hamblin, at the Bowery Theater, New-York.

"THE King comes here to-night." He who could wring
Our hearts at will was "every inch a king"!
For when in life's bright noon the stage he trod
In majesty and grace, a demigod;
With form, and mien, and attitude, and air,
Which modern kings might envy in despair;
When his stern brow and awe-inspiring eye
Bore sign of an imperial majesty;
Then — in the zenith of his glory — then
He moved, a model for the first of men!
The drama was his empire; and his throne
No rival dared dispute — he reigned alone!
"His feet bestrode the ocean! his reared arm
Crested the world!" His voice possessed a charm
To love's, to friendship's, and to classic ears
Like the sweet music of the tuneful spheres:
"But when he meant to quail and shake the world"
His accents were "like rattling thunders" hurled!
Or plead, "like angels, trumpet-tongued," to prove
The worth of freedom, and the joys of love!

Whether he gave ungentle wives rebuke
As simple *Leon* or *Aranza's* duke;
Or tamed (as wild *Petruchio*) the shrew,
Or showed a fiend in the unpitying Jew;
Displayed the wrecks of passion's withering storm,
In stern *Penruddock's* or the *Stranger's* form;
Whether he bade unnumbered victims bleed
"As *Macedonia's* madman or the *Swede*,"
Moved as *Iago*, or the generous Moor,
Or gallant *Rolla* 'mid the battle's roar
Stemming alone the tide of war and death;
Hamlet or *Damon*, *Bertram* or *Macbeth*;
Gloster, *Young Wilding*, *Falstaff*, *Charles de Moor*,
The graceful *Doricourt*, the gay *Belcour*;
Brutus — aye, both the Brutuses of Rome;
Mark Antony, lamenting *Cæsar's* doom,
The proud *Coriolanus*, or the sire
Of sweet *Virginia*; still his soul of fire
With grandeur blazed, to ravish or appal —
He "was the noblest Roman of them all"!

Whether he wore the reckless mien of *Pierre*,
Or the time-scathed decrepitude of *Lear*,
"Fourscore and upwards"— he might justly say:
'Did n't I, fellow? I have seen the day
When, with the very lightning of my brow
I would have made them skip — I am old now,
And these same crosses spoil me."
                              Yes, 't is true,
He once commanded where he now must sue;
For he 's old now — and those unrivaled powers
For you exerted in his happiest hours,

Like flickering lights which in their socket burn,
Are fast departing — never to return!

But shall he now, when silvered o'er with age,
Who never made his exit from the stage
But 'mid the thunders of heart-felt applause,
Unhonored pass, when he at last withdraws?
He who devoted all his noonday powers,
To strew your thorny path with classic flowers —
He, whom with laurels you have thickly decked,
Shall he at last be chilled with cold neglect?
Perish the thought! 't is Cooper's right to claim,
Besides the glory of a deathless name,
Of your regard a more substantial proof
Than the loud cheers which shake this vaulted roof;
Protection for his offspring! dearer far
To his fond heart than earthly glories are;
And you concede this claim — or else, to-night,
Here were not seen a galaxy so bright
Of beauty, taste, and fashion, — 't is a blaze
Which so reminds him of his better days
That fond regrets, with gratitude sincere,
Are mingled in the language of a tear.
And as the worn war-horse at trumpet shrill
Leaps o'er each barrier that restrains his will,
So comes our monarch of a former age
Again to claim his empire o'er the stage,
From tyro potentates this truth to wring:
He *was* and *is* "in every inch a king";
With one bright flash renew th' expiring flame,
And gild the trophies round his honored name.

AN ADDRESS.

Oct. 30, 1834.
Written by Mr. Charles Woodhouse, and read by Mr. Arthur C. Southwick on the occasion of the opening of Histrionic Hall, No. 126 North Pearl Street (then Orchard Street), Albany, New-York.

'TIS said that fashion rules this world of ours;
And true it is we own and feel her powers,
Her sway resistless by this act confess,
In presentation of this night's address.
How like a dream this scene to-night appears?
And is it true, 'midst doubt, and hopes, and fears,
A new and better house we now behold?
Upsprung, as by enchantment, while our old
No more will tell the drama's grief and mirth,
But give that boon to this, whose recent birth
We hail this night with pleasure undefined,
Flowing from every joyful, *grateful* mind.
In ancient Greece the drama claims her birth:
A sacred clime, renowned 'bove all the earth
For Science, Art, and Eloquence, which tells
To present time its spirit-moving spells,
Here on this soil, where the historic pen
Has wrote her epitaph of noble men.

Where deeds of time are writ with impress deep
On tables, their eternal fame to keep;
Here sprung the drama — *here* life's mimic scene
First taught as *Truths* from Fancy's field to glean;

While, like a glass, reflecting e'en the hearts
Of men, the Muses played their magic parts;
Portrayed the passions of the human soul;
Taught us the good to cherish, and control
The bad; placed Virtue in her own bright view,
And painted Vice in every hideous hue!
And thus the stage, if kept in morals pure
(A moving world in moving miniature!)
Still holds a mirror in which all may gaze,
And learn a lesson to direct their ways;
And while we see fair Virtue's cause defended,
Find the amusing with the useful blended.

In this a helping hand we lend; and here
The drama's friends this humble temple rear.
Here shall the Truth exhibit all her charms,
And to black Falsehood sound her dread alarms.
Here shall be cherished all that tends to raise
The mind to soar aloft on Poesy's lays;
The moralists glean ethics for the young,
Clothed in poetic dress, by Fancy sung;
And now, spectators, in your smile so bright
We cheerfully begin this work to-night;
And tho' we hold in the dramatic cause
An humble station, yet, with your applause,
We may our feeble aid lend with success
In showing Life in its most simple dress;
That all may see themselves reflected true
To the image Justice gives of us and you;
And thus transmit, to the remotest age,
A pure and useful Histrionic Stage!

AN ADDRESS.

1834.
Written by Mr. George C. Chase, for the benefit of Mr. Thomas A. Cooper, at New Orleans. Spoken by Mr. George Barrett.

As some bold mariner by storms long tossed,
His all, save hope, in trackless ocean lost,
Steers his frail bark by vivid lightning's glare,
With cheek unblanched, 'midst all the terrors there —
Braving the billows manfully, descries
The wished-for harbor and propitious skies —
He comes to greet you, not the least, if last,
And in your smiles finds balm for sufferings past.
Crowned with a laurel wreath, by friendship wrought,
By you bestowed — as welcome as unbought,
He comes, glad in the memory of hours
Passed in your own bright land of sun and flowers.

'T was his, full often here in times gone by
To strike the chord of generous sympathy;
'T was his to picture forth each noble part —
The high, proud workings of the human heart,
Ambition, jealousy, revenge, pride, hate,
In humble cottage or in princely state.
'T was his with words of fire to move the throng,
And rouse resistance to the tyrant's wrong —

In virtue's cause to mail his manly breast,
And stand forth friend and champion of the oppressed;
Still most admired in honesty arrayed,
For then 't was all himself — 't was COOPER played!

To draw from virtuous eyes a priceless tear
For dying *Brutus* or forlorn old *Lear* —
To wake the terrors of Rome's proudest name,
To catch a gleam from noble *Cato's* flame —
To rule a wife — to tame a wayward shrew —
The melancholy Dane — the cruel Jew —
Aspiring *Macbeth*, red with bloody thought —
Iago's honeyed words with mischief fraught —
The kingly *Damon*, on the scaffold throne —
These, in his day of power, were all his own.
So was the Roman father — and to you
To-night he gives his own loved daughter too.
Receive her kindly from the old man's hand,
And cherish into life this blossom of our land.

AN ADDRESS.

Oct 27, 1835.

Written by Mr. George P. Morris, and spoken by Mrs. Hilson at a benefit given to Mr. Placide in the Park Theater, New-York.

THE music's done. Be quiet, Mr. Durie,
　Your bell and whistle put me in a fury!
Don't ring up yet, sir — I've a word to say
Before the curtain rises for the play!
　Your pardon, gentlefolks, nor think me bold
Because I thus our worthy prompter scold;
'T was all feigned anger. This enlightened age
Requires a *ruse* to bring one on the stage.
　Well, here I am, quite dazzled with the sight
Presented on this brilliant festal night!
Where'er I turn whole rows of patrons sit,
The house is full — box, gallery, and pit!
Who says the New-York public are unkind?
I know them well, and plainly speak my mind —
" It is our right," the ancient poet sung —
He knew the value of a woman's tongue!
With this I will defend ye: and rehearse
Five glorious *acts* of yours — in modern verse:
Each one concluding with a generous deed
For Payne and Dunlap, Cooper, Knowles, Placide!

'T was nobly done, ye patriots and scholars,
Besides — they netted twenty thousand dollars!
" A good, round sum," in these degenerate times —
" This bank-note world," so-called in Halleck's rhymes;
And proof conclusive, you will frankly own,
In liberal action New-York stands alone.
Upon the stage, thirteen brief years ago,
Flush'd with the hopes that ardent bosoms know,
A youth appear'd: nor friends, nor loud acclaim
Ushered him forth. Unheralded by fame
He came among us, with a taste refined,
A vivid fancy, and a burning mind;
Nature his model, counselor, and guide,
The goddess found him ever at her side.
All her instructions he instinctive caught,
And ne'er o'erstepped her modesty in aught
Until the wreath for which he strove was won,
And gay Thalia crowned her favorite son!
 'T was then the public, with admiring eyes,
Saw a new star in placid beauty rise
And take its place, transcendent and alone,
The brightest jewel in the mimic zone!
Though roams he oft 'mong green, poetic bowers,
The actor's path is seldom strewn with flowers;
His is a silent, secret, patient toil —
While others sleep he burns the midnight oil,
Pores o'er his books — thence inspiration draws,
And wastes his life to merit your applause!
Oh ye, who come the laggard hours to wile,
And with the laugh-provoking muse to smile,

Remember this; the mirth that cheers you so
Shows but the surface — not the depths below!
Then judge not lightly of the actor's art
Who smiles to please you, with a breaking heart!
Neglect him not in his hill-climbing course,
Nor treat him with less kindness than your horse;
Uphill indulge him — down the steep descent
Spare, and don't urge him when his strength is spent;
Impel him briskly o'er the level earth,
But in the stable don't forget his worth!
So with the actor — while you work him hard,
Be mindful of his claims to your regard.

 But hold, methinks some carping cynic here
Will greet my homely image with a sneer.
Well — let us see — I would the creature view;
Man, with umbrageous whiskers, is it you?
Ah, no, I was mistaken — every brow
Beams with benevolence and kindness now;
Beauty and fashion all the circles grace —
And scowling envy here were out of place;
On every side the wise and good appear —
The very pillars of the State are here!
There sit the doctors of the legal clan,
There, all the city's rulers, to a man;
Critics and editors and learned M. D.'s,
Buzzing and busy, like a hive of bees;
And there, as if to keep us all in order,
Our worthy friends, the Mayor and the Recorder!

 Well, peace be with you. Friends of native worth,
Yours is the power to call it into birth;

Yours is the genial influence smiles upon
The budding flow'rets opening to the sun,
They all around us court your fostering hand —
Rear them with care, in beauty they'll expand —
With grateful odors well repay your toil,
Equal to those sprung from a foreign soil;
And more Placides bask in your sunshine then,
The first of actors, and the best of men.

AN ADDRESS.

Dec. 8, 1835.   *Written by Mr. Hugh Moore. Spoken by Mrs. John Greene at Mr. William Duffy's Benefit at the Albany Theater.*

FRIENDS of the drama, friends to every part
Of human action that improves the heart —
Friends to the free-born sentiment that blends
Alike the names of rich and poor as friends —
While your good wishes form a wreath of smiles,
To cheer us onward in our path of toils,
Free be the offering that our feelings lend
The drama's patron and the actor's friend.

Friends of the drama, in the ancient time,
When fancy's flower bedecked the wings of rhyme,
When Shakspeare flourished, and when genius hurled
The shafts that pierced the follies of the world—
Then woke the drama from its night of gloom —
A morning sun beamed o'er a moldy tomb.
Oh, may the beam thus snatched from early night
A beacon serve from superstition's night!

From thoughts thus sacred to the " march of mind "
We homeward turn, and leave an age behind
Where erst arose the humble roof, and where
The words of genius wasted on the air,

Now stands the temple of the drama's cause —
Where tyrants tremble, and where bigots pause;
Here, nursed in friendship, Forrest gained a name,
High in the niche of histrionic fame,
And all that cheered him, in his lone career,
'T was *thine* to give — *his* nature to revere.
Thus by thy aim — and long may Duffy prove
That sterling talent merits public love.

Friends of the drama, in a scene like this,
Where patrons smile, *all* language proves amiss,
Save the high tones that gratitude imparts —
The words of friendship gushing from our hearts.
To female beauty, as the brightest gem
That throws its light o'er woman's diadem —
We proffer virtue — as the choicest part
Of *modern drama* in the human heart.
We proffer friendship as a kind behest,
To warm the feelings of the human breast.
We proffer love — nay, ladies, do not start,
'T is but the offering of a grateful heart,
Too full to give the sentiment its due,
When all its magic beams, at once, from you.

AN ADDRESS.

July 3, 1837.   *Written by Mr. Edward Johnson.   Spoken by Mr. J. M. Field, at the opening of the New St. Louis Theater.*

WHEN Freedom's flag was wide o'er Greece unfurl'd,
And Delphi was the center of the world,
The Drama first uprear'd the rustic stage,
To smooth the manners and instruct the age;
And though hoar Time has sped with ceaseless flight,
And crush'd the splendors of that age of light —
Though the famed monuments of that bless'd day
Have fallen to earth, and molder'd in decay —
Though, vision-like, two thousand years have roll'd,
And Greece is not now what she was of old —
The Drama still, to kindly feeling true,
Loves the bright land where first her childhood grew,
Points to her *Thespis*, who, though rude in art,
Touch'd the warm feelings of each generous heart;
To *Æschylus*, who madden'd while he sung,
And o'er the lyre a hand of frenzy flung;
To *Sophocles*, who, gorgeous and sublime,
Lives to this day, and only dies with Time;
And to *Euripides*, whose plaintive song
Seizes the list'ner as it floats along —

Leaves with the bosom liquid notes of woe —
Steals to the heart, and makes the tear to flow!
Where the rough Alps, with summits high and free,
Look o'er the plains of fallen Italy —
The drama there a look of pity throws,
For there, in days of yore, her anthems rose;
For then were heard the mirth and laughter loud
When *Plautus's* muse address'd the Roman crowd;
When *Terence*, too, pour'd forth the comic song,
The cheers were high — the laughter loud and long.
Again she casts her searching eyes around:
"Beware!" 't is whispered, "this is holy ground!"
Why? 'T is on Briton's Isle our footsteps stand,
Nay, it is more — 't is Shakspeare's fatherland!
Here did that master all our feelings scan —
Each nook, each recess in the heart of man;
Here brilliant Sheridan fame's laurel won;
Here, Johnson put his "learned buskin" on.
Flush'd with fond joy, she turns with rapturous glance
To vine-clad hills and sun-bright vales of France;
Points to the theater with tragic mien,
And marks the passions of the stern *Racine*.
For those who pity, and who kindly feel,
She asks a tear — to shed with "*great Corneille!*"
Now, swift across the Atlantic wave she flies —
Where, reared 'mid wilds, her beauteous domes arise!
Each hill and dale her thrilling voice has heard,
And *Forests* echo to the native *Bird;*
Throughout our land, where'er she chance to roam,
She finds a *resting-place* — but here a *home!*

We dedicate to thee, oh! goddess bless'd,
This, thy *first* temple in the far, far West!
Oh! fondly cherish this fair house of thine,
And shed around thy influence benign.
Let vivid images of bygone things
Defile before our eyes like "*Banquo's* kings";
Let *Lear* again enact his frantic part,
And sweet *Ophelia* steal the hearer's heart:
Let the kind audience feel a fond regret,
And weep with *Romeo* over *Juliet;*
Let *Spartacus*, again from bondage freed,
Not like a slave, but like a Thracian bleed;
Picture the scene where chaste *Virginia* fell,
And point to "freedom in the shaft of *Tell!*"
And may the sylph-like nymphs our joys enhance
By mystic trippings of the fairy dance
On Ariel's wing, and soft as brooklet's flow,
Their footsteps falling like the flakes of snow —
Let their lithe forms in mazy circles run,
And grace receive — what Taglioni won!
Let these fair walls with echoes soft prolong
The dulcet gushings of each soul-born song —
Sweet as the euphony of heaven's bright spheres
Strike the bland warblings on the list'ner's ears.
Now to our audience — honor'd, learn'd, and gay —
The humble speaker hath one word to say:
If e'er loathed vice should rear her hideous face,
Or in this tragic fane find dwelling-place —
If e'er this house with scullion jesting rings,
Or desecrated be to sinful things,

Let the bold actor his presumption rue —
Be cursed the player and his temple too.
But if the muse, enlighten'd, never strays
Far from the pleasant path of virtue's ways,
Then shall fair learning sanctify this dome,
And joy and science fix their lasting home —
The tragic muse shall high her scepter rear —
The sternest eye shall glitter with a tear.
Mild Thalia, too, shall all our griefs beguile,
And from the lips of sorrow steal a smile.
The rudest hearts shall feel the genial power,
And future ages bless this natal hour!
Then o'er the player be your kindness shed,
Pour out a golden shower upon his head;
And may this house be ever richly bless'd,
And *stars* arise hereafter in the *West!*

AN ADDRESS.

Dec. 7, 1840.   *Written by Mr. Alfred B. Street. Spoken by Mr. Collenburne at the opening of the Dallius Street Amphitheater, Albany.*

TO lift from age Time's burden for a while,
And light the brow of manhood with a smile,
Repress the tear and hush the sorrowing sigh,
And bid mirth sparkle in the youthful eye;
With Pleasure's golden pinions plume the hours,
And muffle their quick feet with thornless flowers;
Display the wondrous strength and grace that Heaven
To this proud fabric of the soul has given —
The sway despotic, human reason wields —
The tame submission brutish instinct yields;
These are our objects. Is a guerdon due?
Kindness and favor then we ask of you.

Round the wide arena now the fiery steed
Loos'd from his thraldom, bounds with headlong speed,
Free seems he as the tempest, yet a rein
Is o'er him, stronger than the weightiest chain;
An eye and voice whose slightest glance and sound
Plant him a breathing statue on the ground,
Eager and watchful; then their different sway
Shoots him again, an arrow on his way.
With a light leap as upward borne on wings,
To the fleet courser's back his rider springs;

Around — around — the flying Centaur skims,
And to the sight in dizzy circles swims;
Now on his surging pedestal unchecked,
Whirling along, the rider stands erect;
Pois'd with stretched arms, now leans, with sudden bound,
Now to the eye another change is found;
Then, leaping o'er some barrier in his way,
Regains his platform like a bird its spray,
While the gay harlequin in motley drest,
Draws the loud laugh, with gambol quaint and jest.

Fancy flies back to those old classic days
Which witnessed Greece in glory's brightest blaze;
That purple clime, once Freedom's proudest dower,
Cradle of Arts, the Muses' greenest bower,
Again the amphitheater displays
Its splendid pomp to Athens' crowded gaze!
Tier upon tier of animated life
To view the struggling race — the wrestling strife —
The strong athlete grasps sinewy foe,
Muscle strains muscle — blow succeeds blow —
The-foaming courser whirls the chariot on,
And the green laurel crowns the triumph won.

Thus do we strive your cheering smiles to gain
With anxious efforts — shall we strive in vain?
To cast bright drops in life's dark chalice, ours;
To deck earth's desert with a few sweet flowers;
Yours be the meed that all our toil repays
Our gladdening laurel-wreath, the bounty of your praise.

PROLOGUE TO NATURE'S NOBLEMAN.

October 7, 1851. *Written by Mr. Henry Oake Pardey. Spoken by Mr. William E. Burton, at Burton's Theater, Chambers Street, New-York.*

DESPONDING critics oft of late presage
The closing of the histrionic page.
They mourn that Shakspeare, e'en, has lost his power;
That Sheridan has strutted out his 'hour.'
Does not great Horace Greeley plainly say,
We 've grown too wise and good to need 'the play'?
That mind and heart disdain the drama's rule,
And study 's needless in the scenic school?
Thespians arouse! and tell th' erratic sage,
Firm as his printing press we 'll keep the stage.
   The drama languishes. Let us detect —
Polonius like —' the cause of this defect.'
'T is certain that the sprightliest tongue must fail
To win attention to an 'oft told tale.'
We cannot ever with 'crook'd Richard'. fight,
Or weep with Desdemona, every night;
And even cloying is the luscious sack,
If we too often sip with 'burly Jack';
Nor, every week, will people take the trouble
To witness Hecate's cauldron hiss and bubble;

Nor can we, as we have done, hope to draw
Still on 'The Rivals,' or 'The Heir at Law.'
We 've seen sly Jack his father's anger rouse;
We 've heard Lord Dowlas tutored by his spouse.
Old English comedy should now give way;
It has, like Acres' 'dammes,' had its day.
Hang up bag-wigs — our study now should be
The men and the moustachios that we see.
Let us some pictures of the time provide;
Let the pen, practically, be applied!
   Or, shall we seek our stores beyond the main,
When literary freedom we may gain?
'London Assurance' why should we endure?—
Our own assurance should be 'doubly sure'!
The doting Baronet or flimsy Peer
Need not, exclusively, be mirrored here.
Why should the theme of our dramatic sports
Be the amours of kings, th' intrigues of courts?
Can we an interest for *our* stage command
With fancies wove by transatlantic hand?
Thus shadowing forth ' the forms of things unknown '—
Painting all character, except our own?
   Perhaps some of my auditors will cry,
Such reasoning as this will ill apply,
When a high-sounding title you display
In this your so-called genuine native play!
Suspend your censures — you shall be assured
We 'll make a good use of our English Lord.
Who knows but in the pressure of our scene
We 'll make him bend to a Columbian queen?

Peer as he is, we'll try and make the *man*,
By far the better half, republican!
  Do not our author's anxious toil despise:
Judge less by what he does than what he tries.
Two hours your patience — then decide his right
To *have* and *hold* his title of to-night.

AN ADDRESS.

Dec. 20, 1852. *Spoken, and probably written, by Mme. Julia de Marguerittes at the reopening of the Green Street Theater, Albany.*

METHOUGHT my task accomplished — but I find
The part most difficult remains behind.
As yet unseen have I my work performed —
By Science guided, by Ambition warmed;
But now, I must produce myself, poor me,
Who hath not skill, nor science, as you see.
'T was easy to explore the realms of taste,
Thence to evoke the temple you have graced.
The Golden Wand its magic spell hath wrought,
Behold! in these bright forms survive my thought.
And now I come to consecrate the shrine —
To you I give it — 't is no longer mine.
I would but welcome those benignant powers
That blessed the drama in its brighter hours.
Once more let beauty condescend to smile
On the brief pageant and the gorgeous wile;
Once more let gallantry with sense unite,
And cheer us ever, as you 've cheered to-night;
And, if some shadows o'er this picture fall,
The sunshine of your smiles will brighten all.

AN ADDRESS.

Dec. 27, 1855.   *Read by Miss Keene at the opening of Laura Keene's Varieties, New-York.*

ONCE more surrounded by my early friends,
On whom each hope of fair success depends;
I feel impelled — though some may deem me vain —
To cry with joy, " Laura's herself again! "
Night after night, while toiling in the cause
For others' good, your generous applause
Made study pleasure, labor, something dear,
Cherished ambition, and extinguished fear.
Now, for myself, I try my mimic skill,
Anxious my boxes (play and cash) to fill.
Will you assist me with your generous aid?
If so, a grateful debtor twice you've made.
What shall I promise ? — That all things shall be done,
Or new or old e'er seen beneath the sun.
Make up a pie-crust batch, profoundly spoken,
To bear the proverb out — both made but to be broken.
Declare the patent cull'd from every land
Shall at your nod combined before you stand.
Oh, no; excuse me; spite of the classic rhymes,
Which form'd addresses in dull, good, old times,
I'll try the railroad pace of this our age,
And hurry up by steam their slow-coach stage,

Variety is life's best spice, folks say —
That be my aim — my motto, "Ever gay."
Not here shall tragic muse with tearful eyes,
And heaving breasts replete with anguished sighs,
Gaze on her dagger and her fatal cup
As if about on poison still to sup —
No — if she come, unless we toil in vain,
We 'll fill her poison cup with mirth's champagne;
With muses' spells make glad each list'ning ear,
And dance with flying feet away from care;
Do all we can to drive life's gloom away,
And end with joy the labors of the day.
Give welcome to you all. Then let me ask,
Ladies, your smiles to cheer our willing task;
And you — good gracious! what a palpitation
I feel before you, lords of the creation!
Excuse me — was ever anything much more un-
    lucky? —
I have no smelling salt, or e'en a decent bouquet,
Therefore take pity on my sad complaint.
You see ——
I must proceed; with feelings truly Keene
I ask your presence at our festive scene;
An anxious suppliant before you stands —
Shall I succeed? That splendid show of hands
Removes all doubt. Armed in Hope's fear-proof mail
I feel, indeed, there 's no such word as — fail.

AN ADDRESS.

1858. *Written by Judge Conrad, and read by Miss Caroline Richings at the opening of the Philadelphia Academy of Music.*

WHEN Time was young, and Music's spell 't is said
Moved stones and trees, and ev'n recalled the dead;
Then (when the poet's dreams were sooth), the lyre
Once bade a city's prostrate walls aspire;
Quick throbs the granite rock — a living thing;
The ruins tremble with the trembling sting;
They move, responsive to the lyre's command;
They form, they rise, a towery wall they stand.
Such power had Music's self! But lo! A thought —
Her shadow — here a mightier work hath wrought;
Spells of the past here bade the walls arise,
While list'ning Hope lean'd o'er with glad surprise.
Soon towers the dome — the temple soon expands,
For thousand needs quick meet a thousand hands;
The purpose planned, 't is jostled by the deed,
And wonder on wonder crowds with eager speed;
'T is done, and nobly done! Exulting art
Smiles o'er the pile, so perfect in each part:
Wide and harmonious, as bright Music's reign,
Her newest triumph lights her noblest fane:
Long may it stand! — long yield the tribute due
To art, to joys reproachless — and to you.

Music, whose hymns the stars of morning sung,
Ere the sweet spheres by Discord's hands were wrung;
Whose rules great Kepler in the planets saw,
And knew in them the universal law —
The law by which the stars their orbits sweep,
And quivering worlds their course in concert keep.
Music, whose code by bright Ægea's tide
(So Plato tells) overruled all codes beside.
For Athens trembled o'er the Lydian lute,
And Sparta battled to the soft-voiced flute;
Music! whose boundless wealth, like day, can give
At large, unlessen'd unto all who live;
Costless, yet priceless; free as ocean's wave,
Alike to Fortune's darling and her slave;
The peasant's joy, it thrilled Arcadia's sky;
The poet's bliss, it lighted Milton's eye;
The courtier's grace, 't was gallant Raleigh's pride;
The lover's voice, so burning Sappho sighed;
The warrior's summons: when 'mid Alpine snows
Gaul's quick strength faltered and her hot blood froze—
When squadrons fainting, paused, or stark and stiff,
Toppled to gulfy death far down the cliff;
Sudden, Napoleon bids the war charge sound,
And wild and high, the glaciers echo round —
They start, they burn; their nerves are fire again —
They win the height, to conquer on the plain!
Music! which sins not, cannot fail nor fade,
Exalter, friend, consoler, soother, aid!
Here, in her temple, we her altars rear,
And service meet, hearts, hopes — all offer here.

Nor sole, though regnant, here our sovereign sway:
The Drama, too, shall know its better day.
Bright in the splendor of immortal youth,
Rich in rare wisdom, poetry, and truth;
What though her mirror darkling mists distain,
Clear but the surface, it will shine again —
Shine with the wild and weird-like glory shed
By poet-seers, the myriad-minded dead.

In such a home, where ardent service tends,
Where wealth is zealous, and where worth befriends,
No more shall scenes unmeet the stage profane,
Nor vice, nor folly, steal into her train.
Afar the tastes, which with her genius war,
The sullying jest, the sordid taint, afar.
The drama here in vestal fame shall live,
And crave no triumph virtue cannot give.

As when the morn on Memnon's marble shone,
The marble warm'd, breathed music's sweetest tone,
So in your kindling smiles our dawn will break,
And music here in grateful witchery wake,
The buskin'd muse with solemn step descend,
And their sweet spells the arts and graces lend.
We of our temple proud, our triumph too —
Proud of our cause — and patrons, proud of you,
Will call up worlds of faery — pure and bright
With genius, wit, worth, melody, delight —
While white-rob'd Virtue, from her sacred throne,
Smiles o'er the scene, and claims it as her own!

A PRIZE POEM.

Feb. 9, 1863. *Written by Mr. Henry Timrod. Spoken by Mr. Walter Keeble at the Opening of the New Theater at Richmond, Virginia.*

A FAIRY ring
    Drawn in the crimson of a battle-plain —
From whose weird circle every loathsome thing
And sight and sound of pain
Are banished, while about it in the air,
And from the ground, and from the low-hung skies,
Throng, in a vision fair
As ever lit a prophet's dying eyes;
Gleams of that unseen world —
That lies about us, rainbow-tinted shapes
With starry wings unfurled,
Poised for a moment on such airy capes
As pierce the golden foam
Of sunset's silent main —
Would image what in this enchanted dome
Amid the night of war and death
In which the armed city draws its breath,
We have built up!
For though no wizard wand or magic cup

The spell hath wrought,
Within this charmèd fane we ope the gates
Of that divinest Fairy-land,
Where under loftier fates
Than rule the vulgar earth on which we stand,
Move the bright creatures of the realm of thought.
Shut for one happy evening from the flood
That roars around us, here you may behold—
As if a desert way
Could blossom and unfold
A garden fresh as May—
Substantialized in breathing flesh and blood,
Souls that upon the poet's page
Have lived from age to age,
And yet have never donned this mortal clay.
A golden strand
Shall sometimes spread before you like the isle
Where fair Miranda's smile
Met the sweet stranger whom the father's art
Had led unto her heart,
Which, like a bud that waited for the light,
Burst into bloom at sight!
Love shall grow softer in each maiden's eyes
As Juliet leans her cheek upon her hand
And prattles to the night.
Anon, a reverend form,
With tattered robe and forehead bare,
That challenge all the torments of the air,
Goes by!
And the pent feelings choke in one long sigh,

While, as the mimic thunder rolls, you hear
The noble wreck of Lear
Reproach like things of life the ancient skies,
And commune with the storm!
Lo! next a dim and silent chamber where,
Wrapt in glad dreams, in which, perchance, the Moor
Tells his strange story o'er,
The gentle Desdemona chastely lies,
Unconscious of the loving murderer nigh.
Then through a hush like death
Stalks Denmark's mailéd ghost!
And Hamlet enters with that thoughtful breath
Which is the trumpet to a countless host
Of reasons, but which wakes no deed from sleep;
For while it calls to strife,
He pauses on the very brink of fact
To toy as with the shadow of an act,
And utter those wise saws that cut so deep
Into the core of life!

Nor shall be wanting many a scene
Where forms of more familiar mien,
Moving through lowlier pathways, shall present
The world of every day,
Such as it whirls along the busy quay,
Or sits beneath a rustic orchard wall,
Or floats about a fashion-freighted hall,
Or toils in attics dark the night away.
Love,—hate,—grief,—joy,—gain,—glory,—shame shall meet,

As in the round wherein our lives are pent;
Chance for a while shall seem to reign,
While Goodness roves like Guilt about the street,
And Guilt looks innocent.
But all at last shall vindicate the right,
Crime shall be meted with its proper pain
Motes shall be taken from the doubter's sight,
And Fortune's general justice rendered plain.
Of honest laughter there shall be no dearth;
Wit shall shake hands with humor grave and sweet,
Our wisdom shall not be too wise for mirth,
Nor kindred follies want a fool to greet.
As sometimes from the meanest spot of earth
A sudden beauty unexpected starts,
So you shall find some germs of hidden worth
Within the vilest hearts;
And now and then, when in those moods that turn
To the cold Muse that whips a fault with sneers,
You shall, perchance, be strangely touched to learn
You 've struck a spring of tears!
But while we lead you thus from change to change
Shall we not find within our ample range
Some type to elevate a people's heart —
Some hero who shall teach a hero's part
In this distracted time?
Rise from thy sleep of ages, noble Tell!
And with the Alpine thunders of thy voice
As if across the billows unenthralled
Thy Alps unto the Alleghanies called,
Bid Liberty rejoice!
Proclaim upon this transatlantic strand

The deeds, which more than their own awful mien
Make every crag of Switzerland sublime!
And say to those whose feeble souls would lean
Not on themselves, but on some outstretched hand—
That once a single mind sufficed to quell
The malice of a tyrant; let them know
That each may crowd in every well-aimed blow,
Not the poor strength alone of arm and brand,
But the whole spirit of a mighty land.
Bid Liberty rejoice! Aye, though its day
Be far or near, these clouds shall yet be red
With the large promise of the coming ray.
Meanwhile, with that calm courage which can smile
Amid the terrors of the wildest fray,
Let us among the charms of Art awhile
Fleet the deep gloom away;
Nor yet forget that on each hand and head
Rest the dear rights for which we fight and pray.

EPILOGUE TO THE GOOD-NATURED MAN.

May 23, 1870.
Written by Mr. William Winter for Mr. Augustin Daly's revival of the piece, at the Fifth Avenue Theater, New-York.

Sir William Honeywood:

OLD custom bids (we 'll not forego it quite)
An epilogue — before we say good-night;
In which the player, anxious o'er his task,
Your cheer would crave, your kindly verdict ask;
For that reward he 's not ashamed to sue;
What true good-nature is he 'd learn from you.
Speak your kind hearts with hands as kind — because
The play ends well that ends in your applause.

Lofty:

For kindly conduct there 's a simple rule —
The man who serves another is a fool.
A benefactor be, with shrewd pretense,
And help yourself to all — except expense.
Intrude; presume; and let your skill be shown
In minding all men's business but your own.
Life never has the interest that appears
When one has set his neighbors by the ears.
That true good-nature is, beyond a doubt —
Unless the benefactor gets found out.

Croaker:

I am the most good-natured man on earth;
But true good-nature is not found in mirth;
I hate a rattle-brain. Give me the man
Who trouble sees before his neighbor can —
And gives him warning. That's the gracious way —
And just as good in life as in a play.
Hang grumbling bores! But sure it is not rash
To indicate th' inevitable smash.
All 's well to-night; but, three months hence, you know —

Mrs. Croaker:

Where there 's a corn-field always there 's a crow!
Good things grow better by a natural law,
Though forty thousand croaking ravens caw.
Good-nature makes a banquet of a crust;
Aye — notwithstanding man must turn to dust.
A cheerful heart, however life may fare,
Makes gladness gladder, lightens every care.
My doctrine 's simple, but 't is very human,
And means contentment both for man and woman.

Leontine:

Love needs good-nature most — and all the more
Because, except to lovers, 't is a bore.
Parents and guardians, take a hint from this!
Don't see the young ones when they want to kiss;
Don't know what game 's afoot! You 're just as wise
As though you always used your ears and eyes.

Let things drift on, the way they used to do
When you were young and love was young with you.
You strolled, by starlight, under summer trees,
And Cupid used to purr —

    CROAKER:
      And used to sneeze.
    OLIVIA:
None but a bear love's privilege would stint!

    LEONTINE:
I honor wisdom and observe your hint.
       (*Salutes* OLIVIA.)

    Mr. HONEYWOOD:
My views 't were vain to state, because the play
Has shown them wrong and swept them quite away.
I've learned that, to be happy, one must show
The rare and precious talent to say no.
But sure a man with such a prize as this
      (*To* MISS RICHLAND.)
Good-natured must be — in excess of bliss.
How to be genial sure he need not ask,
Since to be otherwise would be the task.
In this discussion, then, I'll take no part;
Fate saves me all the trouble at the start.

    Miss RICHLAND:
A kind good-night! But, ere we part, I'd say —
One loving thought to him who wrote the play!

That rare, sweet genius, great among the great,
Who humbly wrought, and kept no pompous state;
The good, true heart, the noble, gentle mind,
That blessed his age, and lives to bless mankind.
He sowed the seeds of kindness everywhere
With the unconscious bounty of the air.
In him love, beauty, mirth, forbearance blent,
And Heaven disclosed what true good-nature meant.

THE POOR PLAYER AT THE GATE.

Jan. 19, 21, 1871.
Written and spoken by Mr. George Vandenhoff for the Holland Testimonial at Wallack's Theater, the Fifth Avenue Theater, Niblo's Theater, and the Academy of Music.

WISELY good Uncle Toby said:
  "If here below the right we do,
'T will ne'er be ask'd of us above,
  What coat we wore, red, black, or blue."

At Heaven's high chancery gracious deeds
  Shall count before professions,
And humble virtues, clad in weeds,
  Shall rank o'er rich possessions.

So the poor player's motley garb,
  If truth and worth adorn it,
May pass unchallenged through the gate,
  Though churls and bigots scorn it.

The Lord of Love, the world's great Light,
  Made Publicans his care,
And Pharisees alone demurred
  That such his gifts should share.

But still he held his gracious way
    Soothing the humblest mourner,
Nor ever bade one sinner seek
    For comfort "round the corner."

The woman that in sin was ta'en,
    Bowed down with guilt and shame,
Found pity in that breast divine
    That knew no taint of blame.

The Pharisees all gathered round
    To taunt, revile, and stone her,
He bade her "go and sin no more";
    His mercy would atone her.

He raised from death the widow's son,
    Nor ask'd his trade, profession;
Enough for him a mother's faith
    In his divine compassion.

He healed the palsied, halt, and blind,
    Nor left one heart forlorner;
He never bade them go and find
    A doctor — "round the corner."

Some modern saints too dainty are
    To walk in paths like these;
They 'd lock the gates of heaven on woe,
    If they but held the keys.

Occasional Addresses.

The widow's friend asks prayers o'er him
   From whom death's hand has torn her;
The saintly man refers him to
   "The small church round the corner."

What is there in the player's art
   Should close the fount of love?
He who on earth plays well his part
   May hope a seat above.

The lessons he has wreathed with smiles,
   The hearts his mirth made lighter
Shall plead like angels' tongues for grace,
   And make his record brighter!

And though not nearest to the Throne,
   Yet sure the lowliest born, or
The actor in the veriest barn,
   May find in heav'n a corner.

All honor to the little church,
   And to its gracious pastor,
Who in his heart the lessons kept
   Taught by his heav'nly Master!

And when this fleeting scene is past
   To sinner, saint, and scorner,
Let's hope we *All* may find, at last,
   A bright home round the corner!

OPENING ADDRESS.

Dec. 4, 1871.   *Written by General C. C. Van Zandt, for the opening of the Providence Opera House. Spoken by Mr. E. L. Tilton.*

BRIGHT, fairy Puck! swifter than rifle-shot,
   Put round the earth thy girdle, spun of light,
And tie it in a jeweled lovers' knot!
   There by the footlights — on the stage to-night
'Tis done! it swings as musical as chimes
   Of "sweet bells," never "jangling out of tune,"—
A star-beam ladder! how the fairy climbs
   To dress his elf-locks in the mirror moon!
Now, Puck! leap down; don't bump your little head
   On the proscenium; you may break a bone,
Or singe your silver wings, or worse, instead,
   B flat by falling in the big trombone;
Here, take my hand, stretch up on your tip-toe,
   Stop winking at the girls — the men will hiss!
You've lived forever! now I want to know
   What Roger Williams would have thought of this?
Why, when he landed on the Seekonk shore
   The Indians said "*What Cheer?*" and it's but fair
To think if he was with us now once more,
   He'd say "I'll take the best orchestra *chair!*"
For, after his long life, so orthodox,
   His very bones don't fill a *private box.*

Yet I believe that stalwart Baptist bore
   Wit, brightening wisdom, 'neath his thatch of gray,
And would have loved the stage, and cried encore!
   Although he traveled in another way,
Never by *stage* — but made *tracts* on the shore.
   Come, Puck! trot out your memories from their
      cloisters,
These *opening* nights are death to rhymes and oysters.

. . . .

   Throwing up his dimpled heels,
   Turning somersaults and wheels,
   Every feather in his wings,
   Like a song-bird trills and sings;
   Dancing eyes, like diamonds bright,
   Tangled curls of sunrise light;
   Teeth as white as snow-drops are.
   Laugh like music from a Star;
   Cheeks as red as sunset hue,
   Breath like violets wet with dew, —
   Little Puck paints fair and fast
   Mystic pictures from the past.

. . . .

My Lords and Ladies, — for, upon my word,
Each Yankee is a lady or a lord, —
The night was dark, a gale was rising fast,
And Newport's spires quivered in the blast,
When in a little building by the shore,
Half deafened by the equinoctial roar,
A band of players from across the sea
Acted a queer, old-fashioned comedy —
Giving their earnings to sweet charity.

There first upon our fields the buskin trod,
Where beaded moccasins had pressed the sod.
And there, a century since, the fair Muse bore
Her first glad offspring on New England's shore.
Your city has a pleasant pictured page
In history for her annals of the stage,
Radiant with stars.   How brilliant seems, forsooth,
The kingly splendor of the elder Booth,
Whether with tragedy he rent the air,
Or with a tender pathos, rich and rare,
Gave a new music to the Lord's own prayer!
Old men are living now who loved to meet
George Frederick Cooke upon the busy street,
Heard Hackett roar in Falstaff, or perchance,
Finn flash his wit's electric-pointed lance;
Saw Charles Kean's Hamlet, and young Forrest's Lear
And mad Joe Cowell play his pranks so queer;
Heard Conway's voice, who sleeps beneath the wave,
Or Hazard's fire, quenched in an early grave,
Or Charlotte Cushman seem the blood to freeze
In gaunt, prophetic, weird Meg Merrillies.
Here Taglioni whirled in fire-fly maze,
Madame Augusta flashed between the plays,
Or Fanny Ellsler's sweet bewitching glance
Made hearts beat cadence to her airy dance.
And later still, came Howard, Forbes, and Drew;
The Palmer's grassy mound is wet with dew;
Old Pardey's nights were crowned with an encore,
And Varrey "set the tables on a roar."
Grace strode the stage superbly, rich in health,
Now he lies palsied — aid him from your wealth!

Three times the Fire Fiend flung his blazing torch
Against the lintels of the Thespian porch;
Three times the Drama sank in dark eclipse,
The rosy fruit was ashes on the lips!
A truce to memories! we have come to-night
With bursts of music and a flood of light,
To dedicate to th' Histrionic Muse
This splendid temple. Not alone we choose
To garland her white limbs and crown her head
With flowers plucked from the past, but we instead
Would nightly on this mimic stage rehearse
Great thoughts embalmed in purest prose and verse,
And elevate the drama from a trade
To what it was when Shakspeare wrote and played;
Call a glad smile to lips grown white with care;
Show virtue radiant as she is fair;
Act comedies, culled from "the golden age";
Retouch with living hues each master's page;
Call Garrick's spirit from across the sea,
And Siddons, stately Queen of Tragedy.
Then Science, Art, the Drama, linked, will stand
The Sister Graces of this Western Land.

A PARLEY BEFORE THE PLAY.

Sept. 9, 1873.
Opening address written by Mr. William Winter, for Mr. A. R. Samuells's New Park Theater, Brooklyn. Mr. Thomas E. Morris, Manager. (Not delivered.)

A

THE flowers are culled to deck another shrine.

B

Which means — the cards are cut to make a deal.

A

There is a hint of slang in that bad line.

B

But slang is what the people like and feel.
No talk of flowers or bowers is needed here;
No costly wine, but only simple beer.

A

That's a mistake. The time, perhaps, has been
When Brooklyn looked on drama as a sin;
When, rapt in decorous sanctity, this town
Gave the poor Thespian nothing but a frown;
But, stronger since in liberal virtue grown;
She knows his worth and makes his cause her own;

And where your simple beer might once have hit
The taste of sinners, parching in the pit,
You 'll find (or falsely all experience paints),
A different drink is relished by the saints.

B

I stand rebuked.   But what I meant to say
Is that plain words are best about the play.
The flowers of fact are well — but flowers of speech
Are things beyond the common public reach.
The public wants to know, in language plain,
In what way *Morris* means to entertain.

A

He means — if so much truth may here be told —
Chiefly to entertain the public gold.
He courts " returns"; he does not care for bays;
He wants " the solid pudding," not the praise.
Give him full benches and full coffers too,
And all is done that he desires to do.—
I hope these words impress the common ear
As wholly practical, precise, and clear.

B

They do.   But much I grieve your sapient mind
Should deem no worthier enterprise designed
In these fair walls, by taste and beauty reared
To all by genius given and time endeared.
Our theater, certain, must be made to pay,
And with that view he 'll " catch the nearest way":
But — reared in days when worth and wit were prized,
And courtly manners had not been despised:

One of the good old school that made the stage
A mirror and a teacher of its age —
Our *Morris*, yielding every point he can
To modern whim, will keep his simple plan —
And be both manager and gentleman.

A

Your thought is kind and your reproof is fair;
But what I meant, in taking on this air
Of worldly wisdom, merely was to pay
Due deference to the doctrine of the day.
That doctrine is (I do not think it nice)
"Success is all! Succeed, at any price!"
Not ours the error, and not ours the shame!
For public wrong the public is to blame.

B

True! And within these walls 't is understood
That a good public seeks the public good.

A

Here let all harmless pleasure be combined
With noble lessons for the heart and mind.

B

Here let no vicious revelry pollute,
By making youngsters wish to "follow suit";
No vulgar sin, well glossed with specious guile,
Be made angelic, in the Gallic style;
No coarse parade of beauties unrefined
Mock the ideals of the modest mind,

Nor sap the spring that sanctifies this earth —
A manly reverence for woman's worth!

A

But, in their place be shapes and words of power;
   Heroes and heroines of the olden time;
The living manners of the passing hour;
   The frolic *Foote*, and *Shakspeare* the sublime;
The Irish wit, that sparkles as it flies;
   The mirth of France, that bubbles through the foam;
The heartsome English thought, that never dies;
   Beauty of Greece, and pageantry of Rome:
The growth of culture in our own fair land;
   The darts of mind, through war and tumult hurled;
And — sword and lily in her conquering hand —
   Art crowning labor, in the western world!

B

With these if *Morris* strive to entertain,
His worthy work should not be done in vain.
'T is yours to crown, or to withhold the meed;
Doom us to fail, or cheer us to succeed.
Accept our efforts, therefore, to be true
To our belovéd art, ourselves, and you!
Kindle a flame from this suggestive spark,
And make a bright renown for *Brooklyn's Park*.

AN ADDRESS.

Dec. 3, 1873. *Written by Dr. Oliver Wendell Holmes. Spoken by Miss Fanny Morant at the opening of Daly's New Fifth Avenue Theater, New-York.*

HANG out our banners on the stately tower!
It dawns at last — the long-expected hour!
The steep is climbed, the star-lit summit won,
The builder's task, the artist's labor done;
Before the finished work the herald stands,
And asks the verdict of your lips and hands!

Shall rosy daybreak make us all forget
The golden sun that yester-evening set?
Fair was the fabric doomed to pass away
Ere the last headaches, born of New-Year's day.
With blasting breath the fierce destroyer came
And wrapped the victim in his robes of flame;
The pictured sky with redder morning blushed,
With scorching streams the naiad's fountain gushed,
With kindling mountains glowed the funeral pyre,
Forests ablaze and rivers all on fire,—
The scenes dissolved, the shriveling curtain fell,—
Art spread her wings, and sighed a long farewell!

Mourn o'er the player's melancholy plight —
Falstaff in tears, Othello deadly white —

Poor Romeo reckoning what his doublet cost,
And Juliet whimpering for her dresses lost —
Their wardrobes burned, their salaries all undrawn,
Their cues cut short, their occupation gone!
" Lie there in dust," the red-winged demon cried,
" Wreck of the lordly city's hope and pride!"
Silent they stand, and stare with vacant gaze,
While o'er the embers leaps the fitful blaze;
·When, lo! a hand before the startled train
Writes in the ashes: " It shall rise again,
Rise and confront its elemental foes!"
The word was spoken, and the walls arose,
And ere the seasons round their brief career
The new-born temple waits the unborn year.

Ours was the toil of many a weary day,
Your smiles, your plaudits only can repay;
We are the monarchs of the painted scenes,
You, you alone the real kings and queens!
Lords of the little kingdom where we meet,
We lay our gilded scepters at your feet,
Place in your grasp our portal's silvered keys,
With one brief utterance: " We have tried to please."
Tell us, ye sovereigns of the new domain,
Are you content — or have we toiled in vain?

With no irreverent glances look around
The realm you rule, for this is haunted ground!
Here stalks the Sorcerer, here the Fairy trips,
Here limps the Witch with malice-working lips,

The Graces here their snowy arms entwine,
Here dwell the fairest sisters of the Nine,—
She who, with jocund voice and twinkling eye,
Laughs at the brood of follies as they fly;
She of the dagger and the deadly bowl,
Whose charming horrors thrill the trembling soul;
She who, a truant from celestial spheres,
In mortal semblance now and then appears,
Stealing the fairest earthly shape she can —
Sontag or Nilsson, Lind or Malibran;
With these the spangled houri of the dance —
What shaft so dangerous as her melting glance,
As poised in air she spurns the earth below,
And points aloft her heavenly-minded toe!

What were our life, with all its rents and seams,
Stripped of its purple robes, our waking dreams?
The poet's song, the bright romancer's page,
The tinseled shows that cheat us on the stage
Lead all our fancies captive at their will;
Three years or threescore, we are children still —
The little listener on his father's knee
With wandering Sinbad plows the stormy sea,
With Gotham's sages hears the billows roll,
Illustrious trio of the venturous bowl,
Too early shipwrecked, for they died too soon
To see their offspring launch the great balloon;
Tracks the dark brigand to his mountain lair,
Slays the grim giant, saves the lady fair,
Fights all his country's battles o'er again,
From Bunker's blazing height to Lundy's Lane;

Floats with the mighty captains as they sailed
Before whose flag the flaming red cross paled,
And claims the oft-told story of the scars,
Scarce yet grown white, that saved the Stripes and
    Stars!

  Children of later growth, we love the play,
We love its heroes, be they grave or gay,
From squeaking, peppery, devil-defying Punch
To roaring Richard with his camel-hunch;
Adore its heroines, those immortal dames,
Time's only rivals, whom he never tames,
Whose youth, unchanging, lives while thrones decay
(Age spares the Pyramids — and Dejazet);
The saucy-aproned, razor-tongued soubrette,
The blonde-haired beauty with the eyes of jet,
The gorgeous Beings, whom the viewless wires
Lift to the skies in strontian-crimson fires,
And all the wealth of splendor that awaits
The throng that enters those Elysian gates.

  See where the hurrying crowd impatient pours,
With noise of trampling feet and flapping doors,
Streams to the numbered seat each pasteboard fits,
And smooths its caudal plumage as it sits;
Waits while the slow musicians saunter in,
Till the bald leader taps his violin,
Till the old overture we know so well,
Zampa, or Magic Flute, or William Tell,
Has done its worst — then hark! the tinkling bell;
The crash is o'er — the crinkling curtain furled,
And lo! the glories of that brighter world!

(Concluded by Mr. FRANK HARDENBURG.)

Behold the offspring of the Thespian cart,
This full-grown temple of the magic art,
Where all the conjurers of illusion meet,
And please us all the more, the more they cheat.
These are the wizards, and the witches too,
Who win their honest bread by cheating you
With cheeks that drown in artificial tears
And lying skull-caps white with seventy years,
Sweet-tempered matrons changed to scolding Kates,
Maids mild as moonbeams crazed with murderous hates,
Kind, simple souls that stab, and slash, and slay,
And stick at nothing, if it's in the play!

Would all the world told half as harmless lies!
Would all its real fools were half as wise
As he who blinks through dull Dundreary's eyes!
Would all the unhanged bandits of the age
Were like the peaceful ruffians of the stage!
Would all the cankers wasting town and State,
The mob of rascals, little thieves and great,
Dealers in watered milk and watered stocks,
Who lead us lambs to pasture on the rocks —
Shepherds — Jack Shepherds — of their city flocks —
The rings of rogues that rob the luckless town,
Those evil angels creeping up and down
The Jacob's ladder of the treasury stairs —
Not stage, but real Turpins and Macaires —
Could doff, like us, their knavery with their clothes,
And find it easy as forgetting oaths!

Welcome, thrice welcome, to our virgin dome,
The Muses' shrine, the Drama's new-found home!
Here shall the Statesman rest his weary brain,
The worn-out Artist find his wits again;
Here Trade forget his ledger and his cares,
And sweet communion mingle Bulls and Bears;
Here shall the youthful lover nestling near
The shrinking maiden, her he holds most dear,
Gaze on the mimic moonlight as it falls
On painted groves, on sliding canvas walls,
And sigh, " My angel! What a life of bliss
We two could live in such a world as this!"
Here shall the tumid pedants of the schools,
The gilded boors, the labor-scorning fools,
The grass-green rustic and the smoke-dried cit
Feel each in turn the stinging lash of wit,
And as it tingles on some tender part
Each finds a balsam in his neighbor's smart —
So every folly prove a fresh delight
As in the pictures of our play to-night.

Farewell! The players wait the prompter's call;
Friends, lovers, listeners! Welcome, one and all!

SALVE, REGINA!

Nov. 7, 1874.

Written by Mr. Richard Henry Stoddard. Spoken by Mr. Charles Roberts, on the occasion of Miss Charlotte Cushman's Farewell, at Booth's Theater, New-York.

THE race of greatness never dies;
 Here, there, its fiery children rise,
  Perform their splendid parts,
  And captive take our hearts.

Men, women, of heroic mold
Have overcome us from of old;
  Crowns waited then, as now,
  For every royal brow.

The victor in the Olympian games —
His name among the proudest names
  Was handed deathless down:
  To him the olive crown.

And they, the poets, grave and sage,
Stern masters of the tragic stage,
  Who, moved by art austere
  To pity, love, and fear,—

To these was given the laurel crown,
Whose lightest leaf conferred renown
    That, through the ages fled,
    Still circles each gray head.

But greener laurels cluster now,
World-gathered, on his spacious brow,
    In his supremest place,
    Greatest of their great race,—

Shakspeare! Honor to him, and her
Who stands his grand interpreter,
    Stepped out of his broad page
    Upon the living stage.

The unseen hands that shape our fate
Molded her strongly, made her great,
    And gave her for her dower
    Abundant life and power.

To her the sister Muses came,
Proffered their masks, and promised fame:
    She chose the tragic — rose
    To its imperial woes.

What queen unqueened is here? What wife,
Whose long bright years of loving life
    Are suddenly darkened? Fate
    Has crushed, but left her great.

Abandoned for a younger face,
She sees another fill her place,
    Be more than she has been —
    Most wretched wife and queen!

O royal sufferer! patient heart!
Lay down thy burdens and depart:
    "Mine eyes grow dim. Farewell."
    They ring her passing bell.

And thine, thy knell shall soon be rung,
Lady, the valor of whose tongue,
    That did not urge in vain,
    Stung the irresolute Thane

To bloody thoughts, and deeds of death —
The evil genius of Macbeth;
    But thy strong will must break,
    And thy poor heart must ache.

Sleeping, she sleeps not; night betrays
The secret that consumes her days.
    Behold her where she stands,
    And rubs her guilty hands.

From darkness, by the midnight fire,
Withered and weird, in wild attire,
    Starts spectral on the scene
    The stern old gipsy queen.

She croons his simple cradle song,
She will redress his ancient wrong—
    The rightful heir come back
    With Murder on his track.

Commanding, crouching, dangerous, kind,
Confusion in her darkened mind,
    The pathos of her years
    Compels the soul to tears.

Bring laurel! Go, ye tragic Three,
And strip the sacred laurel tree,
    And at her feet lay down
    Here, now, a triple crown.

Salve, Regina! Art and song,
Dismissed by thee, shall miss thee long,
    And keep thy memory green—
    Our most illustrious Queen.

EPILOGUE TO OUR BOYS.

Oct. 23, 1875.
Written by Mr. John Brougham, and spoken at the end of the first production in New-York of Mr. H. J. Byron's "Our Boys," at Daly's Fifth Avenue Theater.

MIDDLEWICK *(to* SIR GEOFFREY *confidentially).*
Our children, sir, are ticklish things to handle;
They can't be molded as you would a candle.
We were both wrong; with customers like these
The bullyragging system ain't the cheese.
When we first twigged as they was going to slope,
We should have tried the vally of soft soap.

SIR GEOFFREY.

Ah, well! the past is gone beyond excuse;
This lesson, though severe, will be of use.
Privation only heightens future joys;
Let 's hope 't will bring success to *both* " Our Boys!"

AN ADDRESS.

May 28, 1877. *Written by Mr. George H. Jessop, for the Dedication of Baldwin's Opera House, San Francisco, California. Read by Mr. Henry Edwards.*

THALIA wept so many bitter tears
   When Shakspeare's spirit winged to other spheres,
And "Jonson's learned sock," untimely doffed,
Was banished from the stage it trod so oft,
That Congreve's sallies could not quite console,
And Wycherley but stained the Muse's stole;
Vanbrugh's broad humor had too coarse a touch,
From Farquhar's jests she turned to hide her blush,
And e'en when Brinsley Sheridan essayed
To flash his sparkle o'er the pensive maid,
She only turned her graceful head aside —
"Alas! with Shakspeare comedy has died."

   Be thankful, ye who loved the comic mask,
That Sheridan relinquished not his task;
That, when an unappreciative town
Turned from the doors, and coughed "The Rivals" down,
One partial failure led not to despair —
The path was open and the field was fair;
Another comedy the wit essayed,
A graceful one — it cheered the drooping maid —

This year of grace 't is just one hundred years
Since "School for Scandal" dried the Muse's tears
And fair Thalia saw, with smiling eyes,
Another school of comedy arise.

  Columbia's tears, a hundred years ago,
Kissed dry by Washington, had ceased to flow;
The weary chances of a fearful war,
Its trials and its triumphs were not o'er,
But victory was hovering o'er the land
Drawn down resistless by a master hand;
And oceans, rivers, continents, and isles
Brightened with joy, and rippled into smiles.

  Thalia looked across the western sea
And saw her smiles returned with sympathy;
The clash of weapons faint and fainter grew,
The scenes of tragedy became more few.
"Come," said the Muse, "the din of death is o'er,
And peace is settling on yon western shore —
Yon shore, the first to greet my new-born smiles
While frowns still lowered on these gloomy isles;
There shall Thalia with her drama roam,
There shall she found her temple, make her home."
So spoke the Muse, and, gently wafted o'er,
Lighted, all radiant, on Columbia's shore.
Here the free homage that our country pays
To wit and beauty, wreathed the ready bays,
And blent their emerald with her locks of gold
And made her welcome warm and manifold;
Till, in America, a world surprised
Beheld the Comic Muse acclimatized.

Hers was no passing visit: she brought o'er
The choicest favorites of her repertoire,
She brought them all — Noll Goldsmith, rare old Ben,
And her last choice and greatest, Sheridan.
The lightest spirits, culled from every age,
Donned the bright sock and gaily trod our stage.

Years passed, and o'er the land from east to west
The Muse's fame is everywhere confessed;
Temples have risen hallowed to her name,
Worthy high priests have well upheld her fame.
What fragrant incense burned before her shrine
When Wallack's genius fed the flame divine,
What pathos, blending with his quiet wit —
A mirthful ripple with a tear in it —
Made Rip Van Winkle's quaintnesses enthrall,
And Jefferson the favorite of all.
How oft have Fox's drolleries appealed
To lips but late from Burton's laughter sealed,
Nor e'er appealed in vain; and, ah! how few
Who e'er have seen him can forget John Drew!
And one kind face and sympathetic tone
Blend with the brightest memories we own,
Collecting all the wit that moves the spheres
Unto their fabled laughter for our ears,
L'Allegro's self, the deadliest foe of gloom,
The friend of all the world beside — John Brougham.

Nor, gentle Muse, doth thine own charming sex
Disdain to grace the wit that it respects,
Since Caroline Chapman's mingled grace and power
Made thy halls bright with gladness many an hour,

And Sophy Edwin, mourned and loved so much,
Whose native archness could amuse and touch
Both pleasantly and gently; nor must we
Forget our favorite, whom we still may see,
And will see often ornament this stage,
Whose sprightly humor trips ahead of age —
Oh, Muse! 't is sure thou art not far removed
From real goodness, since thou art beloved
By Mrs. Judah! Blessed be the art
Whose best exponent has so kind a heart;
And now, to-night, high priestess of thy fame,
Louisa Drew, the heiress of thy name,
How many a golden moment in its flight
She grasped, and, in thy service, turned to light!
By that rare alchemy thou 'st left on earth
Whose touch transmutes our sadness into mirth.

Worthy such temples to thy mirthful state,
Worthy such priests thy shrines to consecrate,
Worthy thine honors, growing year by year,
Thalia, Muse of Mirth, be present here!
One laurel from the circlet on thy brow
Hang in this home we offer to thee now.
Teach us to speak, since liking liking moves,
As Shakspeare would be spoke by one he loves;
Show us the smile thou suffered'st to appear
When Sheridan poured courtship in thine ear;
Thy glamour spread through boxes and through aisles,
Till pleasure dimples every face with smiles,
And all this theater, from pit to dome,
Charm with thy presence, for it is thy home —

Occasional Addresses.

A home not all unworthy of thy heart,
The brightest jewel of the builder's art,
The fairest shrine thy lovers could devise
Wherein to offer thee thy sacrifice.
Deign but a glance — are not the colors bright?
Smile but upon them — they will live in light;
A home, fair Muse, to which thou well may'st bring
Thy drama's heroes and thy drama's king.

  And you, kind friends, whose welcome presence shows
Concurrence in the efforts we propose,
May those your kindly faces often grace,
And grace with joy, the rarely vacant place!
Will you not greet Thalia as she comes,
And give a thousand ringing "Welcome homes!"
And say to us, when tinkling prompter's bell
Shows what we 've done, that we have done it well.
Here, to the portals of the Golden Gate,
Where life is throbbing strong in this young State —
The youngest, fairest daughter of the earth —
Youth's best prerogative we bring you — mirth.
Apollo's bow is not forever bent,
Joy's Easter day must alternate with Lent;
Come, smiling faces and applauding palms,
Come, wit and mirth, the sad heart's only balms,
Have welcome and good wishes in your eyes,
And keep them there to see the curtain rise,
For, Muse, to-night we dedicate to thee
This as thy western home of sterling comedy!

AN ADDRESS.

July 17, 1878.

Written and read by Mr. Daniel O'Connell at a farewell benefit given to Mr. Henry Edwards at the Grand Opera House, San Francisco.

DEAR friend, kind friend, and must we say farewell,
   And break that circle, Harry, which so long
Has held us, brother, in its present spell
   A lovely, faithful, merry-hearted throng?

Death claims his own. We mourn, we pray, and trust,
   And softly praise the dead, but yet we know
When nature summons us again to dust,
   We too, along the drear, dark path must go.

But when we feel that though the sun-rays fall
   Upon us living, though when stars are bright
We gaze above and say, " He now sees all
   The mellow beauty of this summer's night."

Still he is absent, and his cheery voice
   Is lost to us, as if our friend were dead,
Though we may grieve and we, perchance rejoice,
   And he rejoice while we are sad instead.

We know not, for, alas! between us lies
   A barrier our thoughts alone may span,
What matter to us stars or glowing skies,
   Since we have lost, of men, the truest man?

The circle narrower grows. Ah, what is wrong
   In this strange world, that partings are so rife?
For ere are hushed the echoes of the song,
   There comes the dirge, and bitterness of life.

The breeze that creeps through aisles of woodland
      shade,
   When day is done, bringing delicious balm,
The cooling mist that freshens all the glade,
   The wave-borne lights that gleam when seas are calm

Are grand, rich blessings in Creation's plan,
   From the Beneficent who reigns above.
But greater is the love of man for man,
   The love exceeding woman's rarest love.

Such is our love. And never better placed
   Was man's affection, since the Persian youth
Beneath the tyrant's footstool strong embraced,
   Glorying in death for friendship and for truth.

The morning sun that climbs the eastern sky,
   And fades at evening in the crimson west,
Though grand at noon its luster to the eye,
   Its last light is the fairest and the best.

And thus our love, in its meridian heat,
    In all the warmth of its noontide power,
Has never seemed so dear, so sadly sweet,
    As in the twilight of this parting hour.

And now, farewell. Night may give place to dawn,
    And birds sing on, and Autumn crown the land,
But what care we when you, our friend, are gone?
    And but the last grip of your faithful hand

Left as a memory of a golden scene,
    On which the curtain all too early fell,
The sad awakening that succeeds the dream
    Of severed ties; farewell, dear friend, farewell.

EPILOGUE TO NANCY & CO.

May 2, 1886.   *Written by Mr. Augustin Daly. Spoken after "Nancy & Co." at the close of the season, at Daly's Theater, New-York.*

NANCY.

A SPEECH? Alas! This dignified occasion
Confuses all my personal equation;
You quite forget we now should utter nicely
Our thanks and farewells to these friends.

GRIFFING.

Precisely.
A wise reminder, and most aptly made, too.
I'd gush with gratitude, if not afraid to.
But oratoric shame's too great a teaser.

MRS. DANGERY.

You might as well be silent, Ebenezer!
The fuss and bungling you have always shown, sir,
Suggest that you let bad enough alone, sir!

CAPTAIN VAN RENSSELAER.

Here's Keife O'Keife; it would not be surprising
If he were graceful at extemporizing.
Just mention with what sadness we are smitten
At our approaching absence in Great Britain.

Occasional Addresses.

DAISY.
Say no unpatriotic Anglomania
Now prompts us to embark on the Aurania.

ORIANA.
Say London, from Belgravia to Old Bailey,
Can't wean us from New York and Mr. Daly.

BETSY.
Say I 'll be true! Though all foine Piccadilly
Should want me picture as the New York Lily!

MRS. DANGERY.
Please tell them *my* regrets are far from cold ones,
For new friends never take the place of old ones!

BRASHER.
Tell 'em, were our sojourn of long duration,
We 'd turn strikers without hesitation!

STOCKSLOW.
Express, I beg, my little deep emotion
To cross that nauseating little ocean!

GRIFFING.
Tell them my loyalty will not be thinned, sir,
Though asked by Mrs. Guelph to dine at Windsor.
No, not if Oscar Wilde, with joy dismayed there,
Threw me a sunflower every night I played there!

O'KEIFE.
Good gracious! you perplex, amaze and shake me!
For what rare-gifted spokesman do you take me?

I'm neither poet, orator nor preacher,
I'm not Bob Ingersoll, Mark Twain or Beecher.
But if you'd like real feeling wed with fancy,
I'll recommend to you —

     BRASHER.

       Of course, my Nancy!
Come, Nancy, now! Tell something light and trippy,
You know you can. Step forward.

     NANCY.

        Spare me, Tippy!
My heart's brimful. Feel how it beats. Just press it,
Tip, the good-by's *there!*

     ALL.

      Why, then express it!

     NANCY.

We might from Greenland stray to Mount Hymettus,
Yet know you'd never slight us, or forget us!
But if, too rashly on ourselves relying,
Fresh fields and pastures new we now are trying,
If soon our modest banner we unfurl in
Fastidious London or esthetic Berlin —
'T is only that your wealth of generous praises
For foreign conquest our ambition raises.
While still we hope, whatever welcome find us,
For none more dear than those we leave behind us! —
And now — not good-by — *au revoir* is better,
You'll hear from us each week or so by letter;
And if we're found exceptionally able,
No doubt you'll learn it all per ocean cable.

AN ADDRESS.

May 31, 1886. — Written by Mr. George Parsons Lathrop for the benefit of Mr. Henry Edwards, at the Star Theater, New-York. Spoken by Miss Maud Banks.

BETTER than regal pomp and pride
   The power that moves to tears or laughter;
The art whose memories sweet abide
   And make life rich forever after.

Better than art, the soul whose plan
   Makes brotherhood the foremost factor:
A man is all the more a man
   Who figures as a sterling actor.

And so the *true man* on the boards,
   Whate'er he feigns of smiles or sorrow,
Lends to the public from his hoards
   More sympathy than he can borrow.

Such is the friend we greet to-night:
   Complete in skill — his humor blending
With honesty time wears more bright,
   And geniality unending.

There have been Edwards crowned as kings;
  And Harrys, too; but if you tarry,
You'll see this man whose good name rings
  With fame of Edwards *and* of Harry.

Why should I lengthen out my lay?
  I see you 're bent upon a moral.
Agreed! But all I have to say
  Is, crown him with your fairest laurel!

AN ADDRESS.

Aug. 8, 1887.
Written by Mr. T. W. Ball, and read by Mrs. Agnes Booth Schoeffel, as "Audrey," at an open air performance of "As You Like It," at Manchester, Mass.

HERE, by the margent of this summer sea,
    Befitting place, where Shakspeare's self might be,
With the green sward responsive to our tread,
This "brave, o'erhanging firmament" o'erhead,
Where the winds whist to hear our sylvan sport,
Here, where King Oberon might hold his court,
I give you welcome, beauty, youth, and age,
To this, our rustic playhouse, and our stage.

In the great master's time, who made our stage
"Th' applause, delight, the wonder of his age,"
The playhouse all was open to the day;
We only follow, where he led the way.
And so, e'en now, with us shall not be seen
The garish lights, the tawdry, painted scene;
Lend your imagination all its wings
And you 'll forget there ever were such things.
Here they are needless; here, where nature rare
Provides no mimic scene, but all is fair;

The turf our stage, the trees our forestry,
The fleecy clouds our glorious canopy!
To read the master's honeyed page aright
Needs no deck'd cloth, no meretricious light;
What better than the leafy boughs, earth's sod,
For him who best communed with nature's God!
The toil-spent actor, when his work is done,
Seeks for some comfort when the race is run:
Some kind assurance that his latter years
Shall not be bound "to saucy doubts and fears."
He's been a prodigal — that is too true,
Yet only prodigal to pleasure you;
He has been rich in giving joys to all,
Yet, somehow, wealth came never at his call.
Worn out with service, when his day is o'er,
And he can rove the drama's fields no more,
To soothe his cares, to ease his bed of pain,
Is the proud privilege his brethren claim;
Thus, their life's labors done, to give them ease,
We ask from you, for whom they lived to please.

For my dear sisters, and my brothers all,
Who've left their ease in answer to the call
Of broad humanity — your hands I crave —
They ministering angels are who save!
Deal kindly with our faults; we are but human —
E'en like yourselves, we are but man and woman.
Deep in your "heart of heart" let us be sown;
"There if we grow the harvest is your own!"

EPILOGUE TO PYRAMUS AND THISBE.

April 7, 1888. *Written by Mr. Edgar Fawcett. Spoken after "Pyramus and Thisbe" at the close of the season, at Daly's Theater, New-York.*

THESEUS.

THIS looks as if you all had been conspiring
   Against my late commands about retiring.
On tough tradition what bold fool would break spear
By thus absurdly amplifying Shakspeare?

HIPPOLITA.

No modern scribes can in their wildest flights dream
Of giving six acts to Midsummer Night's Dream!

LYSANDER.

Your truth such verdict it were rash to stake on.
What of some new-found version by Lord Bacon?

HERMIA.

Bacon? Oh, no! Our play has gone *so* bonnily.
Why *should* we change it?

BOTTOM.

               Ask Ignatius Donnelly!
No doubt he 'll give some cryptogramic reason
Why our sixth act is not an act of treason.

Occasional Addresses.

QUINCE.

Nay, as we 've all much more than mere suspicion,
It 's but an act of — grateful recognition.

FLUTE.

You make us ladies our quaint robes feel shy in!
They 're not the proper ones to say good-by in!

SNUG.

What of us men, like fancy-clad carousers?
No swallow-tails, white ties, or evening trousers?

DEMETRIUS.

Our friends at this will surely not be staggered;
They know we 're old as — "She," by Rider Haggard,
All fresh from Athens, twice a thousand years back,
And —

HELENA.

      Jest away! It helps to keep the tears back!
These garbs we wear, though Greek enough you find them,
Hide Yankeeland in every heart behind them!
That word "farewell," howe'er our speech convey it,
Seems more American the more we say it!
Each year more bounteous in our memory's garden
Grow friendship's fair forget-me-nots! —

DEMETRIUS.   Beg pardon.

Your metaphor 's a picturesque one, surely;
But don't you speak it somewhat prematurely?
I hate objections by the ears to drag on,
But —

BOTTOM.

Is it yet quite time to bring the "tag" on?
You know a quorum's not a full convention.

HELENA.

Forgive!—Forgive my dull misapprehension
That I, their loyal and devout well-wisher,
Recalled not Mrs. Gilbert, Mr. Fisher.

HIPPOLITA.

One more!

THESEUS.

Yes, one 't were strange of us to slight so!

DEMETRIUS.

Bless me if I know whom.

HELENA.

Our Governor!

DEMETRIUS.

Quite so.

BOTTOM.

True! He whose care has given his name to
The Augustin age we all owe thrift and fame to!
Who's monthly, weekly, yes, even daily near us—

DEMETRIUS.

Don't pun upon his name! He'll overhear us!

BOTTOM.

Good heavens! Why did n't some of you prevent it?
Goose that I was!

DEMETRIUS.

He 's here now to resent it!

MRS. GILBERT.

You see! The Governor 's heard your conversation!

MR. FISHER.

And positively boils with indignation!

MRS. GILBERT.

Still, don't look scared, as though you meant dispersal,
He 'll save all scoldings for our next rehearsal.

MR. DALY.

Bearded like Douglas in his hall, I tender
This once my managerial surrender!
My talents, though you praise them or deplore them
Are powers behind the scenes, but not before them.
Old Nero wished the entire great Roman nation
Had but one head, to meet decapitation!
We wish the indulgent throng we now apply to
Had but one hand our clasp might say good-by to!

AN ADDRESS.

July 30, 1888.
Written by Mr. T. W. Ball, and read by Mrs. Agnes Booth Schoeffel at an open-air performance of "A Midsummer Night's Dream" at Manchester, Mass.

"WHAT, Mrs. Schoeffel!" cried a lovely fair,
　　The freshening sea breeze toying with her hair:
Health on her cheek and beauty in her eye,
Her form all grace and queen-like majesty;
"What, give another play upon the green,
And in the cast your name not to be seen?
Why, 't is outrageous!"　"Season for a while
Your admiration," said I, with a smile,
"Though true it is no player's part I claim,
Rest you assured I 'll get there just the same."
And so I come before you, gentles all,
And bid you welcome.　Surely at my call
You 'll not refuse your heartiest applause
To those who labor here in this good cause.
You, friends, who read our Shakspeare's page aright
And sit in judgment on us here to-night,
Well know the scene of our midsummer play
Is in a wood near Athens made to lay;
Old Athens then, but in the later years
The " Modern Athens," peerless among peers,

Seeks out this wood, well fitting, as I ween,
Again to reproduce the mimic scene;
And you 'll admit — I see it in each face —
That 't is a marvelous convenient place.
What is our object? Still as in the past,
To help the needy; round pain's bed to cast,
With tender hopes and sympathetic care,
All comforts that should have a lodgment there;
Succor the widow and the orphaned child
With open hands and ministrations mild.
And on life's journey to the world above
Twine white-robed charity with arms of love.
For this to-night your presence here is sought;
We barter pleasure for the aid you 've brought.
Be it our aim to fill your hearts with gladness,
And by our " Dream " cause no midsummer sadness.
I, prologue-like, your humble patience pray,
Gently to hear, kindly to judge, our play.

AN ADDRESS AT THE PLAYERS'.

Dec. 31, 1888.   *Written by Mr. Thomas W. Parsons. Spoken by Mr. Lawrence Barrett at the Opening of The Players' Club, New-York.*

LET us crown Edwin. Though he wear
  The crown already of his Art,
Grateful Manhattan's mighty mart
  May well a civic garland spare
For one who hath deserved so well
  Of his whole country, carrying far
And wide the great Enchanter's spell
  Under whose thraldom we all are.
Yet not alone his laurel twine
  With civil oak. The poet's bays
And critic's ivy should combine
  Besides, to speak our actor's praise.
For he hath educated men
  (Who knew none other lore but this),
Making past history live again —
  A lofty mark which many miss!
Through him those rough lads of the West
    That never slept beneath a roof,
    Men from the mountains, tempest-proof,
  Gold-hunters, rugged and untaught,
Feel Romeo's passion heave their breast,
  Or Hamlet's wisdom swell their thought.

Even the great Marlborough, we are told,
   More history learned from Shakspeare's page
Than Holinshed's; nor seems it bold
   To guess that many a sapient sage,
As well as soldier, may have known
   More of mankind from gifted bards
Than chroniclers, though he had grown
   Gray o'er the schoolroom's history cards.

(*To the* PLAYERS.)

Players! I ask your benison for this wreath:
Oh, read the name that here is writ beneath
Approvingly, as of all words the one
Most fit to glorify the sire and son!
Perchance the coming centuries will say,
There was a home by Massachusetts Bay,
Whence children came to keep that flame alive
Which Edwin kindled, and may long survive
Till each America, both North and South,
Shall speak him honor with a single mouth,
And England's language from the Arctic main
To San Rosario's watch-tower hold one reign.

(*To* MR. BOOTH.)

Tragedian, teacher, take the crown
   Where Love her myrtle with our laurel blends:
   These portals open to large troops of friends,
But I behold, to cherish thy renown,
   A line, aye stretching as in Banquo's glass,
   Of thousands following after these do pass.

EPILOGUE TO THE INCONSTANT.

Jan. 8, 1889.   *Written by Mr. William Winter for the revival of the piece, at Daly's Theater. Spoken by Miss Ada Rehan.*

NOTE.—*Mirabel's closing speech is:* "*Fortune! has she not given me mine — my life, my estate, my all, and, what is more, her loyal self?*" *And as a reply to this question Oriana speaks these lines.*

ORIANA:

NOT yet! For, what if Oriana choose
   The crown of all your rapture to refuse?
Through many a maze of folly yet of pain
Her faithful heart has felt your gay disdain.
Shall she not triumph — now the strife is o'er —
And punish him who vexed her so before?
No! take her hand. Her heart has long been yours.
True love in trouble all the more endures!
She 'll cling the closer for the risk she braved
And cherish all the more the life she saved.
There 's naught a loving woman will not do
When once she feels her lover's heart is true.

PROLOGUE TO THE WIFE.

April 7, 1890. *Written by Mr. George Parsons Lathrop. Spoken by Mrs. Berlan Gibbs, at the opening of the Lyceum Theater, New London, Connecticut.*

HERE on the bank side of the Thames we meet,
As on the Bankside Shakspeare used to greet
Old London's audience. But *our* London's *New*,
And this bright theater we owe to *you*.
Long is the path from those far English times
When the great drama rang its morning-chimes:
Blackfriars, the Globe, the Rose, the Swan, the Curtain —
Long since, all vanished. Yet who doubts 't is certain
That, while man breathes, new theaters will rise,
And echo with new words 'neath New World skies?

Good friends, who come to us from work or home
To spend with us an evening, as we roam, —
You *bring* us life, we *give* you life again:
Love, laughter, sorrow, starry pleasure, pain;
The blended hopes and motives; all the gain
Of noble conduct, and the triumph glorious
Wherewith true hearts may crown our days victorious.
Your eager living we in earnest play,
And try to show the laws your lives obey.

So, when we leave you, may our mimic scening
Leave with you some fair thought of life's true
    meaning.
Then shall we be content. And may this place
Long be the haunt of music, mirth, of grace,
And worthy actors' art! Thus, when each year
Rounds out its term, the plays enacted here
Shall form a memory as of seasons mellow
Still closer linking fellow-man to fellow.
And when life's curtain on us all descends,
As we have met, so may we part — good friends!

www.ingramcontent.com/pod-product-compliance
Lightning Source LLC
Chambersburg PA
CBHW030333170426
43202CB00010B/1107